W9-CIK-139

THE ACADEMIC MARKETPLACE

This is a volume in the Arno Press collection

THE ACADEMIC PROFESSION

Advisory Editor
Walter P. Metzger

Editorial Board
Dietrich Goldschmidt
A. H. Halsey
Martin Trow

See last pages of this volume
for a complete list of titles.

THE ACADEMIC MARKETPLACE

Theodore Caplow
and
Reece J. McGee

With a foreword by Jacques Barzun

ARNO PRESS

A New York Times Company

New York / 1977

Editorial Supervision: MARIE STARECK

———◆———

Reprint Edition 1977 by Arno Press Inc.

Copyright © 1958 by Basic Books, Inc.

Reprinted by permission of Basic Books, Inc.
  Publishers

THE ACADEMIC PROFESSION
ISBN for complete set: 0-405-10000-0
See last pages of this volume for titles.

Manufactured in the United States of America

———◆———

Library of Congress Cataloging in Publication Data

Caplow, Theodore.
    The academic marketplace.

    (The Academic profession)
    Reprint of the 1960 issue of the ed. published by
Basic Books, New York.
    Includes index.
    1. College teachers. 2. Universities and colleges--
United States--Administration. I. McGee, Reece Jerome,
joint author. II. Title. III. Series.
[LB1778.C3 1977]   378.1'2'0973   76-55171
ISBN 0-405-10002-7

THE ACADEMIC MARKETPLACE

THEODORE CAPLOW
University of Minnesota

REECE J. McGEE
University of Texas

With a foreword by
JACQUES BARZUN

THE

ademic

arketplace

BASIC BOOKS, INC. · NEW YORK

076081

FOREWORD

Since this book deals with the two fundamental concerns of academic men—their working conditions and their performance ex cathedra—it is likely that the last persons to hear about its existence will be the academic profession. For, as the authors of this study point out, the present customs and desires of that profession enforce upon its members a tradition of secrecy, ignorance, and self-deception which, though neither deliberate nor perverse, is yet remarkable in a social group wedded to the forms of truth.

The observers' point of departure was the current problem of mobility within the academic marketplace. First, what is happening to young and old, competent and incompetent, in the accelerated scramble for positions of prestige and emolument in the college and university world? And second, what is happening to colleges and universities themselves in a period of rapid change? While sorting out fact from legend and trying to discern trends, Messrs. Caplow and McGee had to consider all the working parts of the system—if system it can be called—and to assess their suitability to the professed purpose. Their report on the actualities, the myths, and the consequences of present routines thus amounts to an anatomy of an institution.

Like most anatomies, it does not present a pretty picture. But it makes up by instructive surprises for what it lacks in beauty of surface. We learn, for example, that the chief criteria used in making appointments are prestige and compatibility, but that prestige, which rests on scholarly achievement and not on teaching ability, is judged by a survey of opinion rather than a survey of published work: the printed material gathered or submitted for that judgment is looked at but not read (see Chapter 6).

Again, it has been apparent for some time that teaching was being held in less and less repute as government and foundations were offering more and more junkety means of leading the life of the mind. Our authors first describe the precipitous decline in teaching loads and then explain how this tendency is related to the new seller's market, on the one hand, and to the extravagantly indeterminate structure of the university as an institution, on the other.

This indeterminacy is, of course, partly due to the ignorance that this very study sets out to reduce; but it derives also from the radical ambiguity of a profession in which one is hired for one purpose, expected to carry out another, and prized for achieving a third: teaching, research, prestige are independent variables, besides being incommensurable per se. The upshot is as lively a set of anxieties for the agents and the responsible heads of the institution as one could hope to produce by teasing hamsters in electrified cages. Hence the peculiar governance and subdued restlessness of the American university.

This Ruritanian instability does not mean that there are no typical situations. The observers of 215 departments in the nine establishments here surveyed found enough recurrences to give them hope of being able to generalize and to suggest improvements. Their descriptive chapters are crowned by a long discussion of possible reforms.

So cogent and terse is their treatment of each situation, as it is and as it might be, that I refuse to spoil the authors' work and the reader's pleasure by giving more of the story away. I want only to draw attention to two features of the study—one a necessary limitation, the other an unexpected bonus. The limitation consists in the authors' proper unwillingness to take up the cultural conditions of the repeated failures of mind, ethics, and dignity which they report. Why has the American college and university so little connection with Intellect? At a time when the nation is worried about the haphazard training of its talents, this question must be raised, and it is the question closest to, but not identical with, the one here answered.

The second point to be made is that the question that *is* answered here is answered beautifully. Not only is the temper detached and judicious, the facts well gathered and competently marshaled, but the expression of results is invariably lucid. Those who have suffered toxic reactions from other sociologists' prose can partake of this without fear, and indeed with assurance of positive pleasure. Apart from one or two concessions to the jargon of their specialty, the writers display a verbal elegance which their quoted subjects often lack: the main text is witty, imaginative, and in the best sense worldly. To a foundation, this work is obviously a report; to the authors' colleagues, it will be known as a study; but to the reader, the lucky reader, it will surely seem what it is—a book.

JACQUES BARZUN

Columbia University
May 1, 1958

Acknowledgments Are Due

To the Fund for the Advancement of Education, under the direction of Clarence Faust and Alvin C. Eurich, who generously supported this project and encouraged us in every possible way.

To Clifford Kirkpatrick, Robert Merton, Jacques Barzun, James Lewis Morrill, Malcolm Willey, Samuel Stouffer, Logan Wilson, William Cowley, David Riesman, Malcolm Preston, and Donald Young. Each of them has reflected deeply about academic institutions, and all of them have been generous with counsel to us. Whatever traces of wisdom may appear in these pages are probably attributable to these academic men.

To Robb Taylor, now of the University of Wisconsin, who was the third, and not the least, of our interviewing team and was responsible for much of the preliminary interpretation of the findings.

To Patricia James, whose unfailing competence made the preparation of the manuscript more of a pleasure than a chore.

Above all, to the 418 professors who were our tolerant subjects and to the administrative officers of the ten universities whose cooperation made the study possible. We cannot name them because the confidence under which the interviews were taken is best respected by having the universities, as well as the individual respondents, anonymous. It is a privilege to express our sincere appreciation, together with the hope that the results will seem useful to them.

University of Minnesota　　　　　　　　　　T. C.
University of Texas　　　　　　　　　　　　R. McG.
April 15, 1958

TABLE OF CONTENTS

THE ACADEMIC MARKETPLACE

Chapter I

THE
Background

The methods of social research have been applied by university professors to every important American institution except their own. There is an entire literature on the family as a social institution, another on the business enterprise, much research on religious, governmental, military, eleemosynary, and political organizations, but virtually nothing about the university as a social institution.

Aside from a few pioneer studies of the academic profession, most of the general writings about higher education have not been based upon empirical data. There have been many studies of pedagogical matters—class size, instructional outcome, aptitude testing, and the like—but in these the forms of academic organization have been taken for granted. There have also been many studies of the educational and administrative problems of individual universities, but these usually stop short of useful generalization, and are, moreover, usually held as secret and not fit for publication.

In this chapter, we shall first consider the reasons why the academic profession ought to be studied and then review the principal writings from which ideas have been drawn for the present study.

Reasons for Research

There are two good—and quite separate—sets of reasons for studying the university as a social institution.

The first set of reasons is theoretical. The university is a fascinating specimen of social organization, remarkably unlike any other. Its roots, and some of its rituals, go back to the Middle Ages and beyond, but its principal business is innovation. Its hierarchical arrangements are simple and standardized, but the academic hierarchy includes a greater range of skills and a greater diversity of tasks than any business or military organization. Above all, the university is remarkable for pursuing an intricate program with little agreement about fundamental purposes. It is easy for people to agree that the purpose of a factory is production, even if they disagree violently about methods or about the distribution of earnings. It is not at all easy—as we shall presently see—to determine the fundamental purposes of a university or the relative importance of different activities in contributing to those purposes.

The second set of reasons is practical. The current problems of American higher education are serious and are almost certain to become more serious. Since 1945, universities have grown at an unprecedented rate, with very little structural reorganization, and little improvement of educational or administrative procedures. The growth of the past decade will probably be far surpassed in the next few years. The combined effect of a sharp rise in the adolescent population and a steady increase in the tendency to seek higher education will send enrollments soaring. According to the Fund for the Advancement of Education, ". . . it is evident that college enrollments are likely to reach double their 1954 level sometime between 1966 and 1971." [1]

Enrollment pressure is by no means the whole story, however. The proliferation of new subjects, new facilities, and new services, goes on apace, without much reference to the number of students. Some of the sharpest increases in university budgets and staffs were recorded during the period of declining enrollment which intervened between the departure of World War II veterans from the campus and the arrival of the first cohort of freshmen born during the war years.

With everything in the university doubling or tripling in size, the idea of a linear expansion is manifestly absurd. Even on the present scale of operation most of our universities seem to be outgrowing their organizational structures. There is a crying need for reform, and very little significant reform has occurred. Among other reasons, this is because we do not know enough about how the present system works.

The study of the academic labor market is, of course, only one of several possible approaches. The problem has other facets, of equal or greater importance. We have virtually no information, for example, about such matters as these:

the academic department as a work group,
the effectiveness of university administration,
cooperation, competition, and conflict among disciplines,
the characteristics of the undergraduate population,

[1] The Fund for the Advancement of Education, *Teachers for Tomorrow*, Bulletin No. 2, November 1955, p. 14.

the processes of curricular and professional recruitment,

the conditions of scholarly and scientific creativity,

the appropriate conditions for joint research and for individual research,

restriction of output by intellectual work groups,

the development of new disciplines,

the development of new university services,

the selection of research topics,

the decision-making process in higher education.

The present study was, in fact, planned as an entering wedge. It was intended to demonstrate that academic institutions are amenable to sociological field study—that the natives will tolerate the explorer in spite of his close identification with themselves. (Some of our colleagues expressed grave doubts on this point.)

As a topic, the academic labor market seemed at the outset—and seems still—to be peculiarly appropriate for a first approach to the institutional pattern of higher education. In analyzing the results, we have come to think of the faculty vacancy-and-replacement process as an intersection in several planes. There is an intersection between the career of an individual and the history of an institution. There is another intersection between the local system of the university and the national system of the discipline, and still another between the functions of teaching and research. The competing values by which men judge one another and are judged are thrown into high relief in these transactions.

The practical problems of academic expansion are largely labor-market problems. New buildings and new equipment are subject to some construction lag, but—in the decently long run—they need only to be financed to be brought into existence. The expansion of faculties is quite another matter. First, it is a slow process—a matter of decades rather than years. Secondly, it is something of a vicious circle. Faculties can be expanded only if graduate-school enrollment is expanded, and this—because it imposes a direct and heavy teaching burden—requires a prior faculty expansion in the major graduate centers. Thirdly, although the increase of demand for scholarly services poses a problem for society at large, it presents the academic profession with an opportunity to increase its share of social rewards. The dilemmas of this situation have scarcely been perceived, let alone solved.

Some Prior Perspectives

There are many writings from which we have drawn illumination or comfort, but the concepts used in the following pages to describe the academic institution have been most heavily influenced by a small number of oddly assorted authors.

Earliest of these is Adam Smith, whose *The Wealth of Nations*,[2] published in 1776, contains a section dealing with "the expense of the institutions for the education of youth," and another which discusses the market value of "that unprosperous race of men commonly called men of letters." (We have restrained ourselves with difficulty from entitling this volume *That Unprosperous Race*.) Smith, it should be remembered, was a professor at Glasgow, and financial self-pity seems to have been as much a hallmark of the academic profession two centuries ago as it is today. Professional masochism can hardly fail to relish some of Smith's

[2] Adam Smith, *The Wealth of Nations* (1776), London, Methuen & Company, Ltd., 1904, Volume I, pp. 133-136, and Volume II, pp. 249-253, whence the quotations are drawn.

comments under this heading—for example that "before the invention of the art of printing, a scholar and a beggar seem to have been terms very nearly synonymous."

The Scottish philosopher had some remarkably cogent things to say about faculty salaries, endowments, the conflict between teaching and auxiliary duties, and the respective obligations of teachers and students. His observations against faculty autonomy are realistic and thoughtful:

> "If the authority to which he [the professor] is subject resides in the body corporate, the college, or university, of which he himself is a member, and in which the greater part of the other members are, like himself, persons who either are, or ought to be teachers; they are likely to make a common cause, to be all very indulgent to one another, and every man to consent that his neighbor may neglect his duty, provided he himself is allowed to neglect his own."

But the arguments against authoritative administration are even stronger.

> "If the authority to which he is subject resides, not so much in the body corporate of which he is a member, as in some other extraneous persons . . . it is not indeed in this case very likely that he will be suffered to neglect his duty altogether. All that such superiors, however, can force him to do, is to . . . give a certain number of lectures in the week or in the year. What those lectures shall be, must still depend upon the diligence of the teacher; and that diligence is likely to be proportioned to the motives which he has for exerting it. An extraneous jurisdiction of this kind, besides, is liable to be exercised both ignorantly and capriciously. In its nature it is arbitrary and discretionary, and the persons who exercise it, neither attending upon the lectures of the teacher themselves, nor perhaps understanding the sciences which it is his business

to teach, are seldom capable of exercising it with judgment."

In the nearly two centuries since this was written, the incentives for scholarly activity have seldom been examined, although thousands of pages have been written on the incentives of students. Here, too, Smith comes close to having the last word: "Where the masters really perform their duty, there are no examples, I believe, that the greater part of the students ever neglect theirs."

Charles Horton Cooley was one of the founding fathers of American sociology, and his *Life and the Student* is an altogether remarkable book.[3] At their best, Cooley's reflections have the pithiness of Confucian maxims, even when they deal with the complex and tenuous stuff of social organization. No better appraisal of the academic marketplace has ever been made than in these brief comments:[4]

> "It is strange that we have so few men of genius on our faculties; we are always trying to get them. Of course, they must have undergone the regular academic training (say ten years in graduate study and subordinate positions) and be gentlemanly, dependable, pleasant to live with, and not apt to make trouble by urging eccentric ideas."

> "Institutions and genius are in the nature of things antithetical, and if a man of genius is found living contentedly in a university, it is peculiarly creditable to both. As a rule professors, like successful lawyers or doctors, are just hard-working men of some talent."

> "It is true in university life as elsewhere that early success, as distinguished from eventual fame, usually implies an opportunism scarcely compatible with genius."

[3] Charles Horton Cooley, *Life and the Student: Roadside Notes on Human Nature, Society and Letters*, New York, A. A. Knopf, 1931.

[4] *Op. cit.*, pp. 184-185.

Logan Wilson's full-length study of *The Academic Man* [5] was published in 1942. Some of the situations it describes have been changed by the progress of events, and some of its leading hypotheses have been rejected by subsequent studies. It remains, however, a pioneer work of permanent importance, particularly valuable for its emphasis (seven of its twelve chapters) on the evaluation of prestige. The pertinence of Wilson's approach is shown by the present study, which was not originally oriented to prestige as a central variable; our findings, however, forced us to discuss the marketplace very largely in Wilson's terms. [6] The following descriptions by Wilson might almost stand as a brief summary of our data.

> "The meaning of research is so equivocal that almost any sort of investigative enterprise may be connoted, but academic men ordinarily have in mind the kind of inquiry that yields publishable results. . . . Teachers spend much of their working time in a universe of adolescent personalities, yet only by escaping into the universe of ideas do they attain the most coveted symbols of prestige. . . . Thus, paradoxical as it may seem, professional recognition is achieved through activities engaging a minor portion of the average man's activities."

> "The prestige of the educator is primarily dependent on his students, that of the scholar is independent of his students. The latter performs for an audience of experts, competes with equals, and therefore his prestige and the

[5] Logan Wilson, *The Academic Man:* Sociology of a Profession, London, Oxford University Press, 1942. Reprinted by permission. The quotations are from pages 195, 194, and 172 respectively.

[6] Wilson uses the terms "status" and "prestige" somewhat interchangeably, but he distinguishes clearly between what we would call academic *status*—the rank of a position in a college or other organization—and *prestige*—the estimated standing of an individual in a large social group.

visibility of his achievement are relatively independent of the institution that supports him. Faithful teaching service may leave its marks upon the 'hearts and minds of men,' receive its local rewards, and be the occasion for expressions of esteem at alumni banquets, but unfortunately these do not form part of the higher specie of the professional trade."

"The vast majority of the nation's leading scholars and scientists, it is true, are found in the major universities, and the more promising ones in outlying places are constantly being recruited to them. Moreover, the prestige of research centers is so patent that other institutions, established for quite different purposes, indiscriminately try to simulate the pattern, so that teachers almost everywhere must strain to become intellectual innovators."

David Riesman's Nebraska lectures on *Constraint and Variety in American Education* [7] contain a host of ideas concerning our subject. It is to Riesman that we owe the best description of the prestige ranking of universities and colleges—what he calls the Academic Procession—and of the uneasy adjustment between the local loyalties of each campus and the national interests of each discipline. We have almost unconsciously borrowed a good deal of his terminology, especially in discussing the *discipline*.

"A small-town boy who goes to college may be lifted by that encounter into the wild blue yonder of the mind: a discipline with its national and even international market of ideas, can free him from the ethnocentric nest of home and parish, give him a new past (the traditions of 'his' field) and a new identity. . . ."

[7] David Riesman, *Constraint and Variety in American Education,* University of Nebraska Press, 1956. Reprinted by permission. The quotations are from pages 103-105.

"Yet we have also seen that the emancipation achieved by these disciplinary attachments turns out to possess its own built-in restraints. . . . The disciplines at the graduate level often turn out to be new parishes with impalpable and amorphous—hence anxiety-producing—boundaries; these protect one at once against old prejudices and new facts. Scholars who enter a field because of what it can do for them in career terms (rather than because of what they can do for it) often end up as members of intellectual blocs—gatekeepers insisting on tolls being paid to their fields and their preferred factors from any intellectual traffic."

". . . democracy has also meant that, as we have seen, intellectual and academic careers have been opened to many thousands who would otherwise have been forced by circumstance to remain parochial—and reverential to their 'betters.' The combined energies of these men have pushed knowledge forward in this country with an energy akin to that of business expansion; new fields have been opened and staked out; and universities have moved rapidly to assimilate avant-garde innovations in specialization and in integration. The burgeoning market that results also provides a certain freedom for the professor who has disciplinary and cosmopolitan as well as local contacts, for he can exercise a personal veto power over academic autocracy by going somewhere else. . . ."

Jacques Barzun, in *Teacher in America* [8] and in other statements, argues most forcefully that the academic man ought to be above all a teacher. Although he speaks against the existing trends, Barzun speaks for a great segment of the profession to whom the current insistence on research appears both irrelevant and harmful. No one else has ex-

[8] Jacques Barzun, *Teacher in America*, Boston, Little, Brown and Company, and Atlantic Monthly Press, 1946. Reprinted by permission. The quotations are from pages 201-202.

amined the implications of the rules of the marketplace so carefully. Hear him on the subject of undefined criteria:

"It is not in itself bad to put young men on probation so as to choose the best. What is bad is to wrap up the fact in the pretense of promoting scholarship. The testing period should be an admitted fact and a definite limit of time set to it. . . . This means also that while on the job, they should be told clearly what that job is, and it should be seen to that the job is a manageable one. I shall show later why writing a first book and learning to teach are almost always incompatible occupations; and attempting both under a superior's eye adds to the strain. Moreover, doubt sometimes arises as to whose commands must be obeyed. In one university I know of, a beginner has to consider three separate but overlapping authorities as his boss. They compete for his time as scholar and teacher, and he is bound to dissatisfy at least one of them."

"If we follow him after his dismissal—for argument's sake—the prevailing system still beclouds his future. He leaves a first-rate institution to go to an inferior one. What is he expected to do? The new place hired him chiefly to teach and to teach more classes than he is used to. But unless he wishes to stay in that presumable backwater, he must do something else—engage in research, write books and articles, address learned societies. So that here again he is riding two horses, cheating one more set of students, and striving to achieve what may not be within his gifts."

In the recent report of the Committee of Fifteen,[9] the

[9] Committee of Fifteen (Jacques Barzun, Harvie Branscomb, Paul Buck, Philip Davidson, William DeVane, John Dodds, Clarence Faust, Frederick Hard, Charles Johnson, Roger McCutcheon, Donald Morrison, Whitney Oates, Philip Rice, F. W. Strothmann, C. Vann Woodward), *The Graduate School Today and Tomorrow:* Reflections for the Profession's Consideration, Fund for the Advancement of Education, 1955. The quotation is from page 15.

case for the primacy of the teaching function is put more positively still:

> "We finally argued that the ultimate choice between a life primarily devoted to scholarly teaching and a life primarily devoted to research depends on temperament and inclination, and that, since pure research positions are hardly available to a young man in the humanities and the social sciences, even the future researcher must, as a matter of fact, earn the right to devote himself primarily to his studies by being first, and sometimes for a long time, a college *teacher*."

An unpublished manuscript, W. H. Cowley's monumental "An Appraisal of American Higher Education," [10] has been our principal—and irreplaceable—source of information on the history of the academic marketplace and American higher education in general. It enabled us first to question and then to reject some of the most pervasive of our occupational myths. Again and again, in interviewing professors, we heard reference to false but widely accepted beliefs concerning the supposed decline of faculty autonomy, the decreasing independence of the university from outside control, the growth of interdepartmental cooperation, the decreasing number of major institutions, and the increasing opportunities for women in academic careers. Cowley's writings supply the historical facts on these and many related questions. For example:

> "The professor who taught a single subject in which he had specialized did not appear even at Harvard until the arrival of the 19th century, and in most colleges until almost the end of the century faculty members were expected to teach over the whole expanse of the curriculum—

[10] W. H. Cowley, *An Appraisal of American Higher Education,* Stanford University, 1956, mimeographed, unpublished. 520 pages and appendixes.

and most of them did. For example, Professor Oliver March, a member of the faculty and an important administrator at Northwestern University beginning in 1862, at one time or other during his 37 years there taught mathematics, geology, mineralogy, zoology, botany, chemistry, physics, logic, and Greek." [11]

"European universities have followed two historical patterns of government, the French and the Italian. American colleges see-sawed between the two until the nineteenth century and then chose the Italian. . . . I call it the Italian plan, but we got it from the Scottish universities, which had copied it from the University of Leyden, which in turn had adopted it from the Italian universities. For several centuries after the emergence of the Italian universities in the late Middle Ages, students held all their administrative posts, and the student legislative bodies established regulations governing the fees to be paid professors, the length of their lectures, and the fines to be levied against teachers who came to their lecture halls late, who failed to appear on time, and who taught less well than the students thought desirable. Eventually for a complex of reasons, student control waned, and the civil authorities took over by appointing what we would today call boards of trustees, that is, lay bodies of nonacademic people. They became the governors of both professors and students. . . . We have come to follow essentially the Italian plan in the form that Yale and Princeton in particular copied it from the University of Edinburgh. This scheme gave all the governing power to boards of trustees, professors being in fact hired men." [12]

Some years ago Charles H. Page wrote a brief paper called "Bureaucracy and Higher Education," for the *Jour-*

[11] *Ibid.*, p. 359.
[12] W. H. Cowley, "The American System of Academic Government," an address given before the Western College Association.

nal of General Education [13] which has influenced us far out of proportion to its length. It may be credited—or blamed —for the informal use of ideal types throughout our description of the academic marketplace. It was Page, moreover, who suggested by his description of the academic robber baron [14] the feudal analogies we have not been able to shake off, and which appear without sufficient apology in Chapter 9. Here was Page's description:

> "The robber baron, like the ritualist, is well adapted to his bureaucratic surroundings. But this adaptation takes a completely different form; for, rather than glorifying the routines of collegiate life, rather than making ends of means, he will, when it serves his own ends best, ignore bureaucratic propriety altogether. The ability to by-pass prescribed methods, to avoid consultations or procedures called for by the institution's formal code, to cut red tape, demand enormous skills, the courage of one's convictions, and an intense desire to further one's own ends. . . . If the academic robber baron is to escape disgrace and is to remain within the collegiate enterprise, he must possess a highly realistic knowledge of the academic world, must recognize the functionally strategic relationships in and between the formal and informal structures and must display manipulative ability."
>
> "Robber barons need not be the villains of history; sometimes they are heroes. And this is the case of the academic robber baron as well. If their ends correspond with, or are congenial to, the professed goals of the institution itself, the robber baron may, in fact, become a collegiate saint."

[13] Charles H. Page, "Bureaucracy and Higher Education," *Journal of General Education*, Vol. V, No. 2, January 1951. The quotation is from page 99.

[14] Page, in turn, derived the analogy from Robert K. Merton, who used it in a different context in his *Social Theory and Social Structure*.

In his long essay on *The Domain of the Faculty in Our Expanding Colleges*,[15] John S. Diekhoff combined two viewpoints which are ordinarily found in opposition—emphasis on the teaching function and a defense of specialization.

"The professor of biology is not only biologist, but zoologist; not only zoologist, but entomologist or parasitologist. In some universities his professorship is so designated."

"This kind of specialization is often attacked as 'overspecialization,' as though a biologist were unable to conduct an introductory biology course if he knows more than anyone else about the parasites of freshwater fish. In the same way, the professor of English who is genuinely learned in eighteenth-century English literature is sometimes thought to be incapable of discussing books not written during the eighteenth century. . . . Not even great learning (which is a different thing from specialization) is enough to make a man a good teacher, but neither is comparative ignorance. Any learning helps. No college needs apologize for having too many distinguished scholars. Many colleges ought to apologize for not employing them intelligently."

"The Groves of Academe"

It should not be forgotten, in the course of the following pages, that our sample includes only liberal arts departments in major American universities. The universe of higher education is far wider than this. Cowley [16] distin-

---

[15] John S. Diekhoff, *The Domain of the Faculty in Our Expanding Colleges*, New York, Harper & Brothers, 1956. Reprinted by permission. The quotations are from page 33

[16] *Op. cit.*, pp. 90ff.

guishes major universities, minor universities, liberal arts colleges, technological colleges, teachers' colleges, unitary theological schools, separately organized professional schools, and junior colleges in the academic sector of higher education; but he points out that there are at least seven other types of educational enterprise beyond the level of secondary school, including ecclesiastical, military, civil service, business-industrial, nursing-education, labor union, and proprietary institutions—not to mention foreign universities, or the vast differences of structure that can be observed within each of the foregoing categories. The title of this volume, then, is something of an exaggeration. We are dealing only with one row of booths in the academic marketplace, although, by nearly general consent, the most important. There are vast stretches of uncertainty surrounding the small area about which we have some knowledge.

Thus, for example, there are frequent references in the following pages to the "major league," the "minor league," the "bush league," and "academic Siberia." These florid terms are employed in the absence of any common names for large, familiar sectors of the academic world.

Not only our own data but a great accumulation of other writings provide us with information about the major universities and their departments. We have not been able to discover a single scientifically oriented investigation of a non-major institution. The smaller universities and the independent liberal arts colleges are far too important, intellectually and numerically, to be neglected in this way. Descriptive studies of their institutional patterns are badly needed.

Although the present report does not deal directly with these "minor" institutions, it must take account of them at every turn. As alternative employers, they loom large in the awareness of academic men in the major universities. Their faculties are drawn from the same training grounds and have the same disciplinary affiliations. For want of better information, we have been forced to rely upon personal impressions, a scattering of unsystematic interviews, and even works of fiction. For example, in *The Groves of Academe,* Mary McCarthy presents a vivid picture of a faculty oriented—unlike the subjects of this study—to teaching and to campus affairs.[17]

"For the faculty, as has been indicated, Jocelyn was by and large lotos-land. Those continuous factional disputes and ideological scandals were a form of spiritual luxury that satisfied the higher cravings for polemic, gossip, and backbiting without taking the basic shape, so noticeable in the larger universities, of personal competition and envy. Here, living was cheap and the salary-range was not great. The headships of the departments were nominal, falling, by common consent, to the member with the greatest taste for paperwork. Such competition as there was centered around the tutees. The more ambitious teachers, as everywhere, vied for the better students. . . ."

Previous Research

The first quantitative study of faculty mobility was apparently that of Sorokin and Anderson,[18] who studied the records of four institutions (Carleton, Chicago, Harvard, and Minnesota) and concluded that the rate of turnover, "social metabolism," declines with increasing institutional age and size.

[17] Mary McCarthy, *The Groves of Academe,* New York, Harcourt, Brace and Company, 1951, p. 83. Reprinted by permission.

[18] P. A. Sorokin and C. A. Anderson, "Metabolism of Different Strata of Social Institutions and Institutional Continuity," *Instituto Poligrafico dello Stato,* Vol. 9, Rome, 1931. We have seen only a summary of this paper.

F. Stuart Chapin [19] studied turnover rates for assistant, associate, and full professors at the University of Minnesota for the period 1912–1930. Turnover (measured by vacancies or replacements, whichever figure was smaller in a given year) was considerably lower for the two higher ranks. When the same data were charted in terms of the survival in each succeeding year of the whole cohort of faculty employed in 1912, the proportion of survival in each succeeding year increased with increasing rank. Chapin also gathered data on new appointments and concluded that the essential decision was made by departmental faculty in 60.6 percent of the cases and by administrative officers in the remaining cases.

Another early statistical study, that of A. B. Hollingshead,[20] covered all outside faculty appointments at Indiana University from 1885 to 1937. He found that 43 percent of all appointees during this period were Indiana alumni but that the higher the rank, the lower the proportion of alumni appointments. One out of five appointees had some kind of family connection to the University staff. Friendships were also shown to play an important part in the appointment process. In another place, Hollingshead states that "Indiana may be viewed as a typical state university and the practices which apply to it would not vary greatly from those in other colleges and universities." [21] This can be challenged.

The most thorough account of the procedures of faculty recruitment in a specific university is found in the

[19] F. Stuart Chapin, *Contemporary American Institutions: A Sociological Analysis*, New York, Harper and Brothers, 1935, pp. 151-157. Reprinted by permission.

[20] "Ingroup Membership and Academic Selection," *American Sociological Review*, Vol. 3, No. 6, December 1938, pp. 826-833.

[21] "Climbing the Academic Ladder." *American Sociological Review*, Vol. 5, No. 3, June 1940, pp. 384-394.

Harvard report of Samuel Stouffer and his associates.[22] The central feature of the plan under which Harvard operates is that the recruitment process is partly independent of the occurrence of vacancies. Permanent appointments are allotted to each field according to a schedule of vacancy expectations, rather than actual vacancies. This is known as the Graustein formula. The report indicates elements of both satisfaction and dissatisfaction with the plan. Harvard maintains what is probably the most elaborate existing system of evaluating candidates. An *ad hoc* committee named for each vacancy is charged with the duty of surveying the entire discipline and discovering the best possible candidate. In this way, the fiction of seeking "the best man in the country"—which is often adopted by strong departments—is given full official recognition. The *ad hoc* committee is viewed—as the report indicates—as a protection against inbreeding. Nevertheless, by a happy coincidence, the best possible candidates were found to be already at Harvard for 79 percent of the associate professorships and 88 percent of the full professorships filled in a four-year period.

Gladys Wiggin [23] studied statements of college presidents and prestige ratings of history professors, graduate schools of education, and distinguished scientists to conclude that "faculty participation in selection and appraisal of professors is valuable only to the extent that the faculty are educated to the broad purposes of university teaching." The relationship between her data and this conclusion is not entirely clear.

[22] *The Behavioral Sciences at Harvard*, Report by a Faculty Committee, June 1954, pp. 197-209, especially, "The Recruitment of Personnel."

[23] "Selecting and Appraising Personnel," in Harold Benjamin (ed.), *Democracy in the Administration of Higher Education*, Harper and Brothers, 1950, pp. 129-148.

A number of cogent essays on the selection of academic personnel have appeared in the *Bulletin of the American Association of University Professors* in recent years. Epstein [24] concluded that in nearly all cases in which poor choices are made for faculty and administrative posts, the reason is inadequate investigation. Lee [25] proposed in 1951 that college salaries be vastly increased to increase the recruitment rate of college teachers. Ekman [26] compared the open and highly formal competition for professorial chairs in Sweden to the American procedure, "which often seems to lack even the semblance of uniformity or the ideal of impartiality."

The President's Commission on Higher Education criticized the academic labor market rather sharply for inadequate machinery, lack of planning, and the unwillingness of colleges and universities to exclude extraneous factors and make faculty appointments on merit. The Commission recommended "the establishment of a nationwide clearing house of information regarding personnel needs of colleges and universities and personnel to meet these needs." [27]

Ruml and Tickton [28] have attributed the decline of the

[24] Ralph C. Epstein, "The Technique of Making University Appointments," *A.A.U.P. Bulletin,* Vol. 35, No. 2, Summer 1949, pp. 349-356.

[25] Harold N. Lee, "The Factor of Economic Status in Professional Recruitment," *A.A.U.P. Bulletin,* Vol. 37, No. 1, Spring 1951, pp. 102-110.

[26] Ernst Ekman, "Selecting a Professor in Sweden," *A.A.U.P. Bulletin,* Vol. 41, No. 3, Autumn 1955, pp. 547-551.

[27] President's Commission on Higher Education, *Higher Education for American Democracy,* Vol. 4, pp. 27-56.

[28] Beardsley Ruml and Sidney G. Tickton, *Teaching Salaries Then and Now,* New York, The Fund for the Advancement of Education, Bulletin No. 1, 1955.

relative attractiveness of the academic career to the deterioration of salaries at the top of the profession, and have argued in several ways that present salary levels are inadequate to attract and maintain professors of suitable quality.

Another bulletin of The Fund for the Advancement of Education [29] presents the basic statistics of this market. Among the salient facts are these: The resident instructional staff of colleges and universities increased from 82,000 in 1930 to 190,000 in 1954, and was expected to increase to a figure between 377,000 and 495,000 in the relatively brief period to 1960. The number of academic doctorates conferred increased from about 2000 in 1930 to 9000 in 1954 but was not expected to rise beyond 14,000 in 1970, even on the most favorable projection. In 1953–54, two out of every five full-time faculty members in 637 degree-granting institutions held the doctor's degree, but more than two out of every five were full professors. These proportions are likely to decline in the coming years. The bulletin also shows that in 1949 only about 5 percent of college presidents, professors, and instructors enjoyed incomes of $10,000 or more, compared to more than 40 percent of physicians and nearly 30 percent of lawyers. Indeed, as late as 1953, the average annual earnings of professors and associate professors in large state universities compared unfavorably with the wages of railroad engineers and firemen, respectively.

Woodburne [30] studied faculty personnel policies by visiting forty-six colleges and universities during a five-month period and conferring with four to seven staff offi-

[29] *Teachers for Tomorrow,* The Fund for the Advancement of Education, Bulletin No. 2, 1955.

[30] Lloyd S. Woodburne, *Faculty Personnel Policies in Higher Education,* New York, Harper and Brothers, 1950.

cers in each institution. His report contains chapters on appointments, promotions in rank, salary practices and policies, opportunities in teaching and research, terms of appointment and separation from the staff, tenure and retirement, leaves of absence and conditions of work, staff planning, and organization for staff problems. It is the principal available source for a description of current policies and practices, although, unfortunately, it does not include any numerical data. Woodburne concludes his study with a program of twenty "essential conditions for development and maintenance of an able faculty." Four of these have to do with improvements in canvassing and appointment procedure, three others with separations, and two with long-range personnel planning.

In sum, all of the major problems in this area have been broached and intelligently discussed, but only a few of them have been analyzed in detail and with reference to the organizational context in which they occur.

A final citation will serve to close this brief anthology of the academic marketplace. As we earlier remarked, there have been almost innumerable studies of local problems in local settings, many of them marked by a high degree of skill and sophistication. Few of these studies ever see print; many of them are regarded as secret documents; but in one way or another, they contribute to the slow formation of a common perspective on academic structures, functions, and goals. The collaboration of the authors of this report began with such a local study, and we have drawn as extensively as possible on the experience of others in similar efforts. Perhaps the most distinguished, and certainly the best organized, of these enterprises, has been the Educational Survey of the University of Pennsylvania, under the joint direction of Joseph H. Willits and Malcolm G. Preston.[31] Here are some of the assumptions on which their work began.

"A university is an institution which applies systematic research to almost everything under the sun—except itself. A university's purposes are important enough and complex enough to warrant the most intense study."

"The processes of a university are infinitely subtle and complex. Where processes are complex and subtle, there is always great opportunity for sympathetic self-study and there is always room for almost unlimited improvement."

"The tendency is strong in most universities to expand in more directions than available finances make wise. The resulting poverty is shared by all."

"Universities do not sufficiently distinguish between the very good, the good, the fair and the poor in their ventures and in their personnel."

We have long since adopted these assumptions as our own. They suggest both the reasons for undertaking this study and the practical objectives which we hope to serve. In the next chapter, we turn to a more detailed statement of the problem and the methods by which we approached it.

[31] University of Pennsylvania, *Report of the Educational Survey, The First Year*, June 30, 1955. Reprinted by permission.

Chapter 2

THE
Problem
AND THE
Method

The general purpose of the study was to develop a body of systematic knowledge about the academic labor market. We began with the assumption that what "everybody knows" about it would probably turn out to be inaccurate or incomplete. Hence it seemed well to approach the subject as naïvely as possible, trusting the data to make us more sophisticated.

There were a dozen specific questions to be answered:

1. What are the circumstances leading to faculty terminations?
2. What factors in the academic situation are related to occupational adjustment? How is performance in academic positions evaluated?
3. What are the consequences of alternate forms of department organization for the morale and productivity of faculty members?
4. How do existing patterns of migration meet the conflicting requirements of stability and progress, both for individuals and for institutions?

5. What is the range of existing practices for discovering and evaluating professorial candidates?

6. What are the consequences of various methods of selection for the universities and departments which use them?

7. What factors determine an institution's attractiveness to outside candidates? Do the same elements determine its power to hold its own staff?

8. What are the criteria which govern the ranking of candidates for academic positions?

9. How effective are the current methods of canvassing and recruiting?

10. What is the effect of the prestige ranking of institutions upon the success of their recruiting efforts?

11. What are the principal current trends in academic personnel policies?

12. How is the faculty selection process related to the effectiveness of such academic functions as teaching, writing, public service, and research?

The Unit of Study

The unit used in this study is a *vacancy-and-replacement* involving a full-time faculty position. In other words, our unit is a sequence of events. A typical vacancy-and-replacement extends over months, or even years, and involves many people. It occurs within a large-scale organization, and hence it will be differently perceived from different positions. Consequently, we cannot hope to discover all that might be known about it.

In this study, the subjects are institutions and their component parts. We are analyzing the experience of universities and departments, not the experience of Professors

X and Y. Therefore, we did not seek out the people who had been hired and fired—the "commodities" in the labor market. Our subjects are the people who participated in the vacancy-and-replacement as agents of the institution.

Even with this proviso, the scope of the inquiry is limited. Concerning each vacancy-and-replacement, we interviewed the chairman of the department and a "peer"—that member of the department closest in rank and age to the man who left. Presidents, provosts, and deans were interviewed about general policies and procedures but not about individual vacancies-and-replacements.

To the sociologist, the department is perhaps the most interesting component of the university, because of the extraordinary involvement and commitment of its members. The process by which a department replaces its members and maintains its immortality is as nearly central to an understanding of academic institutions as anything can be. Hence, our emphasis on that part of the personnel process which falls inside the department.

The Sample

Our sample consists of all professorial vacancies-and-replacements which occurred in the liberal arts departments of nine major universities during the academic years 1954–55 and 1955–56. A tenth university was used for the pilot study and for experimentation with interview procedures.

Although there are about 250 institutions in the United States which call themselves universities, the U. S. Office of Education recognizes only 141 as such, and the American Association of Universities includes only thirty-nine. This latter group may be regarded as major institutions.[1] It would have been advantageous, certainly, to have studied all of them, but the sample was chosen to maximize diversity and to represent the range of relevant characteristics. Of the ten institutions:

3 are in the Ivy League
4 are in the Big Ten
1 is in California
2 are in the South
5 are endowed
5 are state supported
5 are in metropolitan centers
2 are in middle-sized cities
3 are in small college towns
3 have degree-granting branches
5 contain more than one liberal arts college
2 have separate colleges for men and women

All ten are undoubtedly *major* universities. Three of the five institutions which conferred the greatest number of Ph.D. degrees in the years 1948–55 are included and, taken together, the universities in our sample account for more than one third of the doctorates awarded annually in the United States.[2]

In some respects major universities resemble one another very closely, but the arrangement of colleges and departments is one of their least uniform features. Although there is surprisingly little variation in the division of knowledge into departmental territories, the list of departments included in the undergraduate liberal arts college is variable. Physics, chemistry, economics, geography, and

[1] We shall use the term "major league" for this same group of universities when the metaphor seems to be appropriate.

[2] W. H. Cowley, *op. cit.*, p. 89ff.

music are sometimes located elsewhere in the university. Social work, accounting, journalism, and education are as often found outside the college as in. In two of the universities in the sample, all departments cross college lines and contribute to both professional and undergraduate instruction.

The working rule used to resolve these discrepancies is that every discipline which in most of the universities in the sample is located in the liberal arts college is included for the entire sample. Any discipline which is not located in the liberal arts colleges in at least six of the ten universities is excluded. Departments in women's colleges are included. Departments in branches are excluded. Departments falling partly inside and partly outside a college boundary are included in their entirety. By these rules, departments of the following disciplines are included in the sample: anthropology, archeology, art, biochemistry, biology, botany, chemistry, classical languages, economics, English, French, geography, geology, Germanic languages, history, home economics, Italian, journalism, literature, mathematics, music, Oriental languages, philosophy, physics, political science, psychology, romance languages, Slavic languages, social work, sociology, speech, theater, zoology.

Each university was asked to list the assistant, associate, and full professors in these departments whose employment terminated between June 30, 1954, and July 1, 1956 —whether by resignation, dismissal, death, or retirement. Strangely enough, obtaining this list was one of the most difficult problems we encountered. In most institutions, records of departed professors are kept very indifferently. Some universities took weeks to assemble the list, and errors were not uncommon.

It should be noted in passing that the criteria of selection apply to the vacancy, not to the replacement. A case was included if it invòlved an assistant professor replaced by an instructor, but not if it involved an instructor replaced by an assistant professor. If the vacancy occurred between the specified dates, the case would be included even if no replacement had been made at the time of the interview.

The pilot study was completed in 1956, and all the remaining interviews were conducted during the first half of 1957. The earliest vacancy included in the study might have occurred almost three years before the date of the interview; the latest, as recently as seven months before. As it turned out, the recall of events occurring in the first year of the sample period was markedly worse than for the second year, and it is doubtful whether satisfactory results could have been obtained for any longer period.

Part of this problem is attributable to the turnover of chairmen and peers. If the department chairmanship had changed hands since the vacancy-and-replacement, the former chairman was interviewed if he was still on the scene. When the former chairman was not available, the present chairman or acting chairman was interviewed. In almost every case, the incumbent of "the chair" had a fair amount of information on the matter. The situation was less favorable regarding peers. Where these had disappeared from the scene, their successors could not usually tell us very much about the vacancy-and-replacement.

There were a total of 237 vacancies listed in the nine institutions. We were able to obtain interviews from department chairmen concerning 215 of the vacancies, although in 51 cases, either no replacement had been made at the time of the interview or none was contemplated. Peer interviews were obtained for 162 cases, being omitted

for the rest either because the departed member had no
close colleagues or because no peer of his remained on the
scene.

The Interview Schedule

The schedule of the interview consists, for the most
part, of open-ended questions intended to elicit extensive rather than simple responses. The schedule was re-
vised five times. Experience with earlier versions indicated
that improvements could be made by changing the wording of questions, by removing questions which had shown
low yield, and by adding items—such as the department
self-rating—for which a need was discovered.

Certain of the questions were designed to elicit attitudes rather than reports of behavior and were always
asked in the same way. Some questions were subject to
such minor changes of phrasing and arrangement as facilitated the interview.

The interview schedule, which was used for both chairmen and peers, consisted of several parts: first, a section
about *people*—the person who left, the person who replaced
him, and the persons who were interviewed; second, a section on *the vacancy*—how, when, and why it occurred, and
what its immediate consequences were; third, a section on
the search—what sort of canvassing effort was made, for
what sort of position, and with what success; fourth, a section on *the replacement*—how the candidate was found,
evaluated, and appointed. A final section included the interviewer's narrative report of the interview situation, the
department self-rating, and miscellaneous information.

The answers were recorded as nearly verbatim as possible on the face of the form, rechecked by the interviewer

immediately upon leaving the interview, and transcribed on the typewriter by the interviewer before the end of the following day. In scores of cases, the responses overflowed the allotted space, and extra pages were required.[3]

The median length of the interview was slightly less than one hour. Interviews with chairmen tended to be slightly longer than interviews with peers.

Entree and Acceptance

Early in the summer of 1956, a letter was sent to the presidents of ten universities to request approval for the inclusion of their institutions in the study. "The purpose of this study," said the letter, "is to develop a body of systematic knowledge about the academic labor market." There was no suggestion of practical advantage to the institution. A copy of the project outline was enclosed.

The presidents of the five state universities all responded promptly and graciously, in each case referring us to a dean, vice-president, or provost to work out the details.

The five endowed universities proved somewhat less responsive. One of them—counted among the greatest in the world—never answered the letter and, in a later personal interview, its president refused to countenance any study conducted by persons who were not alumni. Another president refused participation for technical reasons. These universities were replaced by two others with similar characteristics.

The three remaining private institutions required rather elaborate explanations and assurances but eventu-

---

[3] The theory underlying this interviewing procedure is discussed at some length in Theodore Caplow, "The Dynamics of Information Interviewing," *American Journal of Sociology*, Vol. 62, No. 2, September, 1956.

ally gave consent and full cooperation. At one of them we were requested to avoid any discussion of salary matters.

Toward the end of the study, the dean of the arts college in one of the state universities objected to the inclusion of "controversial" cases in the sample but subsequently withdrew his objection.

There was no formal procedure for seeking the consent of the faculty as a whole. On each campus, however, we were fortunately able to enlist the active intellectual collaboration of a senior faculty member who was interested in the subject of the research, and inquiries as to the *bona fides* of the investigators were occasionally referred to this person.

In three of the private institutions, a letter over an administrative signature was circulated to the faculty, informing them of the nature of the study, and introducing the investigator. At two other institutions, some official mention was made of the project in staff meetings. Happily, the letters were phrased very neutrally, with no suggestion that the investigators had been invited by the local administration. The announcements created no great stir. Most of the respondents had neither a clear image of the project nor—as far as we could determine—any special predisposition toward it. On the other hand, the fact of administrative approval was almost always explicit and must certainly have affected responses to some extent as compared, let us say, with a study conducted under the auspices of the American Association of University Professors.

An individual, of course, had no obligation to allow himself to be interviewed, but the refusal rate was favorably low. Of more than four hundred persons approached for an interview, seven refused categorically, and ten to fifteen others offered excuses which we suppose were polite refusals. Yet, curiously enough, acceptance of the study was not quite so uniformly good as this account suggests. For a minority of those who were approached—both administrators and professors—the project apparently presented a dilemma. As academic men, devoted (how zealously, the later pages of this report will show) to the idol of research, they find it almost impossible to disapprove of an academically respectable study and wilfully to withhold their cooperation. But, also as academic men, they are far more likely to be skeptical about sociology (if they are social scientists) and about social science (if they are humanists or physical scientists) than laymen would be. Moreover, as professionals in research, they are far more likely to depreciate a particular piece of research which comes under their observation. To some of our respondents, we appeared to be trespassing across academic boundaries. In the circumstances, their cooperation meant more than may appear on the surface.

Some trace of these complex reactions may be found in the interviewer's rating of each subject's receptivity and the informational yield of each interview. These ratings, made at the close of the interview, are presented on a four-point scale in Table 2.1.

Coding and Tabulation

The merits of "open-ended," or narrative, questions are that they do not force the responses into an irrelevant frame of reference and that they allow unforeseen events and attitudes to be reported just as thoroughly as those which are anticipated by the interviewer. The great disadvantage, of course, is that a collection of data obtained in this fashion does not lend itself to easy quantification. The schedule does contain a number of items which call for numerical responses—for example, salary, years of service, dates, and

Table 2.1
Interviewer's Ratings of
Respondent Receptivity and
Informational Yield, in Percent

	RECEPTIVITY			YIELD		
	Physical Sciences	*Social Sciences*	*Humanities*	*Physical Sciences*	*Social Sciences*	*Humanities*
Excellent	7	11	5	6	4	1
Good	74	74	83	59	66	69
Fair	14	11	6	23	21	19
Poor	5	4	6	12	9	11
Total	100	100	100	100	100	100

the number of candidates considered. Most of the items, however, must be converted from qualitative to quantitative form.

One of the authors has been experimenting for several years with various coding systems for data of this kind. The system used in this study draws heavily upon the following findings from those experiments.

A. With adequate training and practice, a satisfactory level of reliability (test-retest consistently exceeding .95) can be obtained in the quantification of narrative data by a team of three coders. Two of these work independently; the third compares their work, identifies discrepancies, and attempts to obtain unanimity on discrepant items.

B. If data are capable of being scaled by coders, a four-point scale is usually most satisfactory for reliability of coding and ease of manipulation. Most of the items in this study were coded on a scale like this:

$$0 \quad 1 \quad 2 \quad 3 \quad 4 \quad X \quad Y$$

X stands for no response, and Y for an uncodable response. This scheme adopts itself to both continuous and dichotomous categories. Thus, academic rank is coded:

    0—Instructor
    1—Assistant Professor
    2—Associate Professor
    3—Full Professor
    X—No information
    Y—Uncodable—*e.g.*, Lecturer

Answers to the question "Is he satisfied with his new position?" are coded thus:

    0—No, extremely dissatisfied
    1—Apparently not
    2—Apparently so
    3—Extremely satisfied
    X—No information
    Y—Uncodable—*e.g.*, "ambivalent"

C. Data which cannot be presented in scalar form are best handled by a binary arrangement without weighting. Thus, answers to the question "Who was consulted before the offer was made?" were coded by simple check marks in the following column:

Participants	Item #30 check
Trustees	————
President	————
Provost	————
Dean	————
Asst. Dean	————
Chairman	————
Whole Department	————
Superior Colleagues	————
Peers	————
Inferior Colleagues	————
Special Committees	————
Standing Committees	————
Campus Formal	————
Campus Informal	————
Outside Formal	————
Outside Informal [4]	————

Similar columns are provided for other stages of the replacement process, from the first steps taken in canvassing for candidates to the welcoming reception for the new staff member. When these columns are compared on the code sheet, a readable profile of the entire procedure appears.

Because of limited resources, the data from the code sheets were analyzed by hand tabulation. Transferring the

[4] These items are cryptic only in appearance. "Outside Informal," for example, means "Professional people from other universities informally consulted about the appointment."

code sheet material to IBM or to edge-punched cards would have permitted more exploration of relationships and might be desirable at some future time.

In sum, the methods used were the simplest which would serve. Experience has shown many ways in which they might be improved if the findings of this study are sufficiently useful to justify further work along these lines.

Chapter 3

How
Vacancies Occur

The presentation of findings in the next few chapters follows the general outline of the interview schedule, which —it will be recalled—proceeds from the vacancy to the search to the replacement. Two chapters will be devoted to each of these categories. We begin here with a general description of how and why vacancies occurred in the liberal arts departments of our sample of major universities in the academic years 1954–55 and 1955–56.

Mobility and Academic Rank

Table 3.1 describes the sample of faculty vacancies by rank and cause. The largest group of vacancies—57 percent of the total—is caused by resignations. The next most frequent causes are dismissals and retirements, with 17 and 16 percent respectively. It should be noted that an unknown number of dismissals are disguised by kindness as ordinary resignations. When we combine resignations and dismissals into the single category of "moves to other jobs," they account for 74 percent of the total number—a proportion large enough to demand explanation beyond the truism that the academic career is marked by high mobility.

The top row of Table 3.1, showing resignations, invites closer examination. What kind of mobility occurs in each rank? The rank most heavily represented in the sample is that of assistant professor, with 47 percent of the total. This would be expected, since most universities employ more

Table 3.1

Rank of Vacancy by Cause of Termination

Type of Termination	Assistant Professor	Associate Professor	Full Professor	Total Number	Percent
Resignation	60	32	31	123	57
Died	2	6	13	21	10
Retired	4	5	26	35	16
Dismissed	34	2	—	36	17
Total	100	45	70	215	
Percent	47	22	31		100

assistant professors than any other rank, and their mobility is likely to be the highest. Most universities have some sort of "up or out" system, to assure the eventual dismissal of their less competent assistant professors; simultaneously, the search for talent subjects the more promising ones to a continuous bombardment of offers from other institutions. Promising young men were probably in greater demand than usual during the period of the study because of a relative shortage of men of established reputation.

Associate professors are under-represented in our sample. The associate professor is usually a man of proven worth, with tenure, and is not subject to the hazards and the occasional vagaries of the "up or out" system. Normally, however, he is not a man of such reputation that other universities will seek him out with tempting offers in the way that a full professor of national or international reputation may be sought. The assistant professor is concerned with bettering himself anywhere he can, whereas the associate professor sees his best advantage in getting promoted where he is.

The full professor, although much less mobile than the assistant professor, is more mobile than the associate professor. Going, as a rule, only upward in his discipline, he is not subject to the constant shifting and squirming of assistant professors and, with appropriate reputation, he is in considerable demand. Any hint of his willingness to move may immediately elicit a number of offers. From his protected postion, the full professor may solicit offers more openly than the associate professor, who has his promotion to worry about. However, he will have fewer opportunities than the assistant professor, for whom "up" is a much larger territory.

In sum, for the assistant professor, both free and compulsory mobility are maximized. For the associate professor, both are minimized: the former by the advantages of immobility, and the latter by the protection, such as it is, of the tenure system. For the full professor, compulsory mobility is at an absolute minimum—although he may be, and occasionally is, fired in the sense suggested by the military maxim "No, they can't *make* you do it, but they can make you damned sorry if you don't!" Free mobility is always possible—but always limited by what the market has to offer.

Mobility and Age

Table 3.2 provides some answers to the question "When do men leave?" by showing the number of years of employment by the university at the time of termination. The percentage given with the modal range is the proportion of vacancies in each rank falling within that range.

Although the modal number of years in employment is identical for all three ranks, the median and the range are instructive. The range of service represented by the

Table 3.2

Length of Service by Rank of Vacancy

	YEARS EMPLOYED			AGE AT MOVE	
	Mode	*Median*	*Range*	*Mean*	*Median*
Assistant Professor	6-10 (27%)	4	1-30	37	34
Associate Professor	6-10 (46%)	7	2-20	45	42
Full Professor	6-10 (31%)	15	6-52	55	57
All ranks	6-10 (27%)	6	1-52	45	43

assistant professors in the sample is 1 to 30 years, the median is 4, suggesting correctly that the larger proportion of cases fall below the modal figure. For associate professors, the median falls within the modal categories, suggesting that the cases are rather evenly distributed on either side of the average. The median term of service for full professors is 15 years, with a range from 6 to 52, suggesting that most serve longer than the modal category.

One of the findings of the pilot study is of particular significance here. At the institution studied, there was, prior to World War II, a statistically significant relationship between the age and salary of full professors. Between 1945 and 1950, the relationship was not maintained. After 1950, there was an inverse relationship between the age and salary of full professors. These findings are not easy to interpret in the absence of further reliable salary data, but they suggest that the salaries of younger full professors have recently become more responsive to the labor market than the salaries of older full professors, regardless of their eminence. It appears that young men are paid more than older men in an accelerating market because the latter, generally speaking, are less mobile for social and psychological reasons. What happens to academic men who become too old for their ranks?

The antiquated assistant professor usually quits his job or gets thrown out of it. From a major university, he may either go to an institution of lesser eminence, where he is given a higher rank, more commensurate with his age, or he may leave the academic profession entirely.

The associate professor who finds himself too old for his rank and peers may either go to a smaller institution or remain where he is as an associate professor until the end of his days, probably being respected by his students and ignored by his colleagues.

The older full professor, if he is unhappy in his department or if his department is unhappy with him, may be in serious trouble. His mobility is highly limited. From the standpoint of the hiring institution, there are many anxieties attendant upon hiring him. Because of his rank, he will be expensive. Because he must be hired on tenure, he will be permanent. Because he is in his declining years, he may fail to produce the quantity and quality of scholarship that is expected from a man of his rank and salary. Yet, on the other hand, if his eminence is so great as to make the risk of such failure worth while, he may be so identified with the department from which he comes that his transfer will reflect no glory on the new university. Once he reaches a certain point of seniority, then, his *po-*

tential mobility declines sharply. The data seem to place this point at about twenty years of service, or about fifty years of age.

Mobility and Institutional Prestige

Having considered who moves and when, let us examine now some of the characteristics of the departments involved. As we have noted, the institutions sampled in this study were some of the major universities of the nation, whose names are household words to every literate citizen. At one point in each interview, the respondent was asked to rate the reputation of his own department in its discipline as being: (1) among the first five in the country, (2) better than average for major institutions, (3) average for major institutions, or (4) poorer than average for major institutions.

The most striking finding is that the chairmen of 51 percent of the departments sampled believed their departments to be among the top five in the country in their disciplines. We have named this phenomenon the Aggrandizement Effect and defined it as a tendency for group members to assign unrealistically high ratings to their own groups in comparison with competing groups. It is not unique to this study and has been observed in many organizational settings.

The Aggrandizement Effect has some interesting characteristics. It appears to displace only the rater's own department. Ratings given to other departments in the discipline tend to agree with ratings of those departments given by other members of the discipline, except, of course, those given by members of the other departments in question. This is to say that ratings of department quality made by men who are not members of the departments rated will tend to concur in the ordering of those departments. It is only when an individual's ratings include ratings of the quality of both his own and other departments that distortions occur. There is no evidence that the amount of distortion is a function of the "real" quality of the department. The upward shift appears to be nearly universal, and therefore, when self-ratings only are compared, they are not totally unrealistic. Severely qualified, they can be viewed as an indication of the approximate quality of the department. On this assumption, we observe that 51 percent of the total mobility encountered in our sample occurs in departments rated by their chairmen, "among the first five in the country," that 36 percent occurs in departments rated "better than average for major institutions," and that only 13 percent occurs in departments rated "average" or "poorer than average."

We may now attempt to answer a more pressing question: *Why* do academic men change jobs?

Involuntary Termination

The involuntary termination, because it is dramatic in a feeble sort of way, is perhaps more interesting than the voluntary resignation. Reference to Table 3.1 indicates that there were 36 firings—that is to say, dismissals admittedly involuntary. The reader is again reminded, however, that, of the 123 cases labeled as resignations, some were probably dismissals disguised by the common administrative practice of allowing a faculty member to resign and "keep his record clean."

Examination of the data discloses a number of reasons for involuntary termination. Perhaps the most common and widely recognized cause is the "up or out" system. This policy is standard in the major universities, although the ruthlessness with which it is enforced seems to vary considerably. The basic formula is as follows: A staff member is employed by the university for a maximum number of years (commonly five, six, or seven). At the end of that period, he must either be promoted "up" to tenure status, which usually comes with the rank of associate professor, or his employment is terminated and he goes "out." Almost everywhere, the severity of these rules is mitigated by provisions for granting tenure to assistant professors who are unable to meet promotion requirements, usually for lack of the doctorate, but who are on other grounds, such as excellence in teaching or possession of special skills, worthy of permanent appointment. Such exceptions are routine in some institutions and extremely rare in others. The criteria by which men are evaluated for tenure appointments are many and varied. A quotation from an interview illustrates the workings of the system and some of the standards applied.

> "He was let go two years ahead of time. His appointment was a mistake. He was dilatory, unreliable and erratic, brilliant, charming, and versatile. But he was in the basic sense unreliable. He showed little inclination to become a scholar. He came to us highly recommended from one of the great universities but he lacked drive and perseverance. We told him that there would be no future for him here and gave him two years to find a new job."

Dismissal may result from such perceived traits as simple incompetence, social ineptness, or a quarrelsome disposition. Judgments of "immaturity" appear with some frequency. Evaluations of this kind also appear in many cases of voluntary termination in our sample. Accidental superfluity also places a small number of men from the major universities on the job market each year. Terminations for this reason reflect no discredit on the individual, and the department may express considerable regret about his loss. Again a quotation from an interview may be illuminating.

> "He was a gifted painter, but we also had one in an associate professor who was a better teacher. There isn't any doubt about his technical competence, but his promotion was blocked by this other man. The chairman felt it was unfair to hold him back from promotion. The decision to let him go was made in January."

A closely related reason for termination is the insufficiency of institutional resources when a man is favorably regarded but the budget does not provide funds for his permanent appointment. The following quotation refers to a case of this kind.

> "He was brought here from one of the big West Coast universities just after he finished the Ph.D. He was here two or three years and then there was a department meeting and he was recommended for tenure. We made the recommendation to the Dean unanimously. The Dean's view was that there was not sufficient student load to sustain another tenure position. We were all in agreement that he was a good man and we should offer him another three-year term as assistant professor, but while we were discussing it he got the offer from one of the smaller midwestern universities."

Another form of involuntary termination, more common than professors like to admit to themselves, is firing by the administration. These cases often become *causes celébres,* and academic men have their folklore about the local incidents on their campuses and are made familiar with the major national ones by the *A.A.U.P. Bulletin* and the press. The Loyalty Oath controversy of 1949–52 at the University of California is an example in point. The quotation which follows speaks for itself.

"I found out in April when we got the budget; that was the first we knew: his name wasn't on it."

The whole problem of the relationships between academic departments and their administrations, and between administration and the individual professor will be explored at length in Chapter 9.

Dismissal sometimes takes the form of a refusal to grant leave. Since this often results in resignation, the termination is technically voluntary. Nevertheless, the refusal of leave, although fairly rare, is a most effective device for accomplishing the removal of a professor with tenure.

Termination on prejudicial or discriminatory grounds, usually those of race or sex, seems to be rare, and our sample includes no cases in which a department member admits that a colleague was dismissed on this basis. Discrimination of this kind is far more likely to occur in hiring, and it is plain at a few of the departments studied that "only white Protestant males need apply."

Our sample does not happen to include any dismissals for political belief or affiliation, but these do occur and are well-documented in the literature on academic freedom.[1]

Rules about "inbreeding" and "outbreeding" also account for a fair number of involuntary terminations, the former being far more common than the latter. "Inbreeding" refers to the hiring of graduates to teach in the same department in which they obtained their training. It is commonly disapproved but widely practiced. "Outbreeding" is characteristic of only a few of the nation's great universities and is a sort of mirror image of inbreeding. It consists in hiring the graduates of other institutions for junior

---

[1] See, for example, Robert M. MacIver, *Academic Freedom in Our Time*, Columbia University Press, New York, 1955.

posts only, so that tenure appointments may be reserved for one's own graduates after they have been seasoned elsewhere. It is usually defended by the theory that having held even a temporary position in so eminent a faculty will be an asset to a man throughout his career. That this makes for high mobility among assistant professors goes without saying.

Nonpromotion as a cause of involuntary termination is similar in effect to the refusal to grant leave. Among tenured associate professors, it often results in resignation. Unlike the refusal to grant leave, however, where administrative considerations may be the major issue, it operates solely through psychological mechanisms. The associate professor who was one of four assistant professors promoted at the same time is unlikely to remain in the department when the other three are given further promotion and he is left behind. The quotation below, from an interview regarding the vacancy left by an associate professor, illustrates the point.

"I could see that he was dissatisfied in May, when he was informed he wasn't being promoted. He quit in June without any warning, I'm sure he wouldn't have if he'd received the promotion. He resigned without any position in hand and went to California."

Even more subtle than nonpromotion, as a device for getting rid of unwanted department members is the "sale down the river," in which a department arranges an outside offer for one of its own members and then persuades or subtly forces him to accept it. This device also functions by pressure on the professional ego, to which most professors are extremely sensitive. A man will seldom linger in a department whose members are unanimously urging him to go elsewhere. A sale down the river lies behind most department efforts to inform a member about other positions, regardless of the altruistic, morale-centered explanations that are offered. The quotation below is typical.

"We helped him get the job he got; we thought it was a good one and we couldn't do that well for him. Teaching and museum work at one of the lesser Ivy League colleges. We heard of it and I worked to get it for him—we couldn't stand in his way. They wrote around and I wrote them that he fitted their needs."

The essential elements of a sale down the river are an unusual degree of initiative on the part of the department and the presentation to the helpless candidate of a *fait accompli*.

Scandal is another familiar reason for involuntary termination, but only two cases were reported in the sample, although several others were discussed. If the small talk of the profession is to be believed, scandals resulting in terminations almost always involve sexual offenses against undergraduate students. (Graduate students presumably are able to take care of themselves.) Although there are stories on every campus about the professor (of either sex) who seduces his students (of either sex), there are few tales told of the professor who patronizes call girls or is "repeatedly" arrested for disorderly conduct.

In connection with involuntary terminations, we should distinguish two kinds of dismissal in terms of their outcomes. These are dismissal from the profession, which results in the choice of a different career by the person dismissed, and dismissal from the major universities, which means exile to the academic Siberia of minor colleges and universities, from which few men return. The quotations below illustrate, respectively dismissal from the academic profession and exile to Siberia. Of the 43 individuals in our sample who were fired or forced to resign, 26 went to other academic institutions (20 of them to minor ones) and 17 went to nonacademic employment (8 to industry or business and 7 to government).

> "He was seeking a job; he was blocked for promotion because he didn't publish. It was no secret that he was looking. He went to a corporation that makes atomic hardware."

> "We had decided not to recommend his promotion. He didn't have enough research promise, although his teaching promise was good. But we decided not to carry him—there was some difference of opinion on that. We notified him at the same time he received an offer from a little Catholic college in the midwest. They were very anxious to get him. I haven't seen him much since then."

Voluntary Termination

Another reference to Table 3.1 will show that resignations or voluntary terminations accounted for 57 percent of the total mobility in the sample. As with involuntary terminations, the data show a variety of reasons for such terminations. The reader is again reminded that these are rough categories and are not presented as exhaustive or absolute. In general, it may be said that voluntary terminations occur: (1) because of discontent and discord within the department, (2) upon the reception of an unbeatable offer, (3) through a "drifting away" process, and (4) for nonacademic, personal reasons.

The theme of discontent and discord is a common one in the academic profession—so common that departmental feuds are regarded as normal and one does not have to pry very far into the history of almost any department to find one. Feuds frequently result in individual mobility—if not a general exodus from the department as the wounded and vanquished leave the field. The quotation below, concerning the vacancy left by a full professor, illustrates the theme.

"It was all concerned with another man who was, in fact, a pretty nasty character: hostile, aggressive, *mean*. But he was a Harvard man and my friend felt, not without some justification, that he had the Dean's ear and was pouring malicious tales about the department in general and himself in particular into it. He may well have been right. Anyway, he felt that he had lost both the respect and support of the administration through the machinations of this man and, since he gave no sign of leaving, my friend decided that he had to."

The unbeatable offer appears in three themes or variations: (1) the Bound to Rise theme—the subject outgrows his university to the point where his own prestige overshadows that of any position which may be offered to keep him there, (2) the El Dorado theme—some special factor, such as climate or cultural setting, assumes such importance to a man that he will make any sacrifice to attain it, and (3) the Silver Cord theme—the university at which the subject took his degree has the power to recall him at any time, often at some material loss to himself. The Silver Cord is, apparently, one of the marks of a *great* university; no man in the sample heeded the call back to Sleepy Hollow State College, but there were numerous instances of men being drawn back to Chicago, Columbia, and Harvard. Such a man returns, apparently, not because he is lured by money or prestige but because the university to which he goes is the one where he was trained and feels most at home and where he can fulfill the ambitions he held in graduate school. The three themes are about equally common. The following quotations show examples of each.

"He'd been offered the deanship of both the Arts College and the Graduate School here and rejected both; he'd simply outgrown the job."

"He and his wife never liked the climate here. She was a native of the West Coast and they both had lived there and wanted to go back sometime. He was actively looking for a position out there from the time he arrived here. He got an offer from one of the big schools there while he was on leave from here at another university in the same general area."

"It was Chicago. He'd done both his undergraduate and graduate work there. The Dean said, 'It was a return to the womb.' He'll find the girl he was in love with twenty years ago has changed a little; her hair is a little gray now and is thinning, and she's heavier than she used to be."

Another cause of voluntary termination is "drifting away" from the department—the situation in which a man's ties with his colleagues become more and more tenuous as he becomes psychologically, and almost always physically, estranged from it, until one day there are no ties left. This drifting away is characteristic of: (1) men doing research which takes them away from their home bases for periods of years; (2) ex-administrators who attempt to return to their pre-administrative scholarly pursuits to find themselves unknown in their old departments (and often unwanted as well); and, (3) men who drift upward into administration, first serving on advisory committees, then acting as consultants, and finally becoming full-time officials.

A final category of voluntary terminations involves personal motives and covers a variety of situations—common and uncommon, comic and tragic—often so inextricably entangled with one another that specific instances become difficult to categorize. Some 22 percent of all the voluntary terminations in the sample involved personal elements.

The Lure of Money

When it was mentioned in the course of an interview that one of the questions to be answered by the study was why professors leave one job for another, the respondent usually laughed and said something to the effect that the answer was obvious—they leave for better salaries. It can hardly be disputed that differences in salary have something to do with the process of academic mobility, but the details of the relationship are not obvious at all.

When the interview reports are analyzed thematically, the appearance of salary themes exhibits a curious pattern: Only 18 percent of the departed men were reported to have been dissatisfied with their salaries when in place, but 58 percent of them were reported to have been attracted by a better salary in the new position they accepted elsewhere. Similarly, only 21 percent of the replacements are reported to have been dissatisfied with their former salaries, but 48 percent of them are said to have been attracted by the offer of a better salary. We must conclude either that academic men are singularly contented with their economic situation—happy with what they have but willing to accept better—or else that the reports are distorted by institutional expectations. The first alternative, that professors are happy with their wages, can be rejected out of hand by anyone acquainted with this milieu.

The matter is somewhat clarified if we compare the leading factors of dissatisfaction and attraction for the four positions involved in each vacancy-and-replacement. For each category of positions, their order of importance, measured by enumerating those cases in which the factor appeared as a theme in the interview, is shown in Table 3.3.

Table 3.3

Reported Dissatisfactions of Former Incumbents (vacancies *)
(The percentages of incidence are shown in parentheses.)

First:	Personal problems	(26)
Second:	Opponents	(25)
Third:	Opportunities for advancement	(17)

Reported Dissatisfactions of New Appointees (replacements *) with their previously held positions:

First:	Opportunities for advancement	(44)
Second:	Work duties	(30)
Third:	The employing institution	(23)

Reported Attractions of New Position Elsewhere for Former Incumbents who were Hired Away:

First:	Salary	(58)
Second:	Work duties	(36)
Third:	Location	(32)

Reported Attractions of Position for New Appointees:

First:	Opportunities for advancement	(58)
Second:	Salary	(48)
Third:	Rank	(30)

* The term "vacancy" will be used when necessary to refer to the *person* who left the position with which the interview was concerned. The term "replacement" will be used in the same way to refer to the person who was hired to fill the vacated position.

The forms of collective self-justification stand out very clearly here. The departure of men who leave the department voluntarily is attributed primarily to their personal problems and personal relationships and thus it reflects no discredit on the reporting department. The departure of replacements from their former place of employment is attributed in good part to the prestige advantages of the new position and thus reflects credit on the reporting department. The attraction of positions elsewhere for men who were lured away from the department are all objective —salary, duties, and location. There is very little perception of prestige advantages in the new position, and comparisons which might be detrimental to the reporting department are avoided. Finally, the inducements which the department believes itself able to offer to new recruits are perceived in terms of both prestige advancement and practical advantage, which presents the reporting department in the most favorable possible light. It is within this complex and highly subjective frame of attitudes that the lure of salary must be described.

The range of practices with regard to salary secrecy in our sample is wide, extending from one university where the salary scale is set by law and colleagues, knowing each other's length of service, can estimate one another's salaries to the dollar, to an equally reputable institution where department chairmen do not always know what salaries are paid in their own departments. Both these extremes are unusual, but some measure of secrecy is normal and expected. In actual fact, salary differentials among the universities sampled are not very great. The exaggeration of salary differentials in discussion is common everywhere, probably in large part as a result of salary secrecy.

It is common academic practice to maintain secrecy about salaries, both within the university and between universities. There are two general arguments for salary secrecy: first, that only through secrecy about individual salaries and salary scales can merit be adequately and speedily rewarded; and second, that department morale would be threatened if members knew what others received, because rivalry would be enhanced by such knowledge. Two opposing arguments are immediately obvious: salary secrecy permits administrative favoritism for departments and individuals to go unchallenged, and secrecy itself creates departmental discord because gossip and speculation fill the vacuum created by ignorance.

The significance of an academic salary is not adequately measured by how many potatoes it will buy.[2] Rank has a great deal to do with the way in which salary is viewed and the kinds of behavior which may be expected concerning it. The assistant professor is likely to measure a given salary by whether he can live on it—as he frequently is not able to do. He may be so accustomed to weighing his salary in potato terms that any proffered increase seems like a turn for the better. He may make a move for the sake of a slight increase in salary which is more than offset by moving expenses and higher costs of living in the area to which he goes. He seldom takes such elements as sales and income taxes into consideration and sometimes does not even investigate the cost of housing and transportation.

For full professors, on the other hand, salary has considerable symbolic significance. Most professors will not live much differently on a salary of $14,000 than on one of $10,000, but the difference between the two figures is nevertheless immensely important to the recipient. At $10,000 he is receiving average pay for his rank at a major university. At $14,000 he is one of the highest-paid scholars

---

[2] In a recent empirical study, Mack is able to show that people in what he calls a determinate occupation (engineers) tend to define their goals in nonmonetary and prestige terms, whereas those whose occupations are indeterminate (salesmen) tend to measure their achievements in income units. Raymond W. Mack, "Occupational Ideology and the Determinate Role," *Social Forces,* Vol. 36, No. 1, October 1957.

in his discipline. He may put the surplus in the bank for his grandchildren, but he is a different man as a result of it.

A peculiar result of the symbolic significance attached to academic salaries is the frequent demonstration by respondents in the interviews that nonacademic salary does not count in assessing academic prestige. Thus, a man who leaves a salary of $9000 derived wholly from his university position and comprising his total income to go to an academic salary of $8000, with the guarantee of an additional $5000 in consulting fees is regarded as having taken a $1000 salary cut and thereby suffers a prestige loss. The quotation below, concerning a professor who moved from a university salary of approximately $10,500 to a "better" position illustrates the other side of the same coin.

> "His salary is $12,000—although he lost a consultantship to the city here which paid him $5000 a year, so he is actually netting less total income—but he has much greater freedom in teaching and research. It's a better job."

Information Screens

It is apparent that reliable information about the academic labor market is, in general, not available to the men who operate in that market. There are many *information screens* [3] within the academic profession which either prevent the dissemination of information entirely or so distort it in passage that it becomes thoroughly unreliable. A number of standard locations for such screens can be identified. Those which came to light in the course of our interviews included:

[3] An information screen may be defined as a set of social practices, beliefs, and behaviors within an organized group which inhibits the communication of certain kinds of information between certain positions or in certain directions.

1. The information screen surrounding reasons for departure. There are few cases of vacancies in which the chairman and the peers agree in detail on the reasons for the departure. There are many cases in which they violently contradict each other and many in which no department member has any idea why a former colleague decided to leave the department.

2. The information screen surrounding the term and conditions of the new position which a former colleague accepted elsewhere. When details are offered in the response, they are usually inaccurate. The number of respondents denying all knowledge is very large.

3. The information screen which obscures the subsequent career of an individual from the department he leaves. Men who resign from academic departments have enlisted in the legion of the lost, as far as their former colleagues are concerned. Although they continue in the same discipline, write for the same journals, and attend the same professional conventions, the amount of information obtainable about the departed individual's career after his departure is very slight. In some mysterious way, he has ceased to be an object of interest to his former friends.

4. The information screen surrounding the official activities of seniors in the hierarchy. The opacity of this screen may be estimated by observing those few departments where it does not exist, so that decisions are made in democratic council. Most of the departments, and all the higher administrations, we observed operate behind information screens upheld by the men of senior rank. One of the most frequent answers to questions in the peer interview

was: "I don't know; it was all decided by the full professors."

5. The information screen erected by departments to hide their hiring procedures from administrative inspection. The common practice is for the department chairman, acting with the knowledge of the tenured members of the department, to propose the name of a candidate to the dean of the college. The candidate's qualifications are usually explained in some detail, but it is a rare department which fully discloses the procedures by which he was selected. He may have been chosen simply because he could be hired easily, or his candidacy may have been the result of a prolonged and arduous sifting process; the Dean has no way of finding out.

6. The information screen erected by the university's administrative officials to shield from the working members of their departments the criteria by which men are officially evaluated. Our data abound in complaints from professors that they were not told exactly either why a given colleague was hired or fired or what he had or did not have that someone else had or did not have. Every university has its legends about certain firings or about recommended promotions that were never made. A haunting minor theme in the interview reports is a story like this [not an actual quotation]: "He was one of the best young men we had, brilliant, productive, an excellent teacher, highly recommended, and unanimously supported by the department. When he came up for tenure, he was fired. We never knew why."

Like salary secrecy, information screening also results in the invention of mythological information on matters of interest when reliable knowledge is lacking. Myth-making seems to be most common in junior peer-groups in the academic hierarchy. The use of a double sample in this study was based partly on the expectation that a man's peers would know more about the details of his departure than would his chairman. In general, they appeared to know considerably less. And in the absence of information, they make myths. Many of these myths to explain unexplained phenomena are standard and widespread. The brilliant young man who meets all of the criteria for promotion, but who gets fired; the dean who has telephones tapped; the fabulous outside offer with a 100 percent increase in salary are twice-told tales. Experienced professors can supply illustrations almost endlessly.

One prevalent academic belief which has passed the stage of myth and may be described as a value assumption of the profession is that a new job is always, in the case of voluntary terminations and often in the case of nonvoluntary ones, better than the old. The reader will recall a possible explanation for the belief that one's colleagues do not leave *because* they are dissatisfied with their salaries. To admit that they do is to raise the possibility that one's own salary may be too low also. Similar distortions occur, as we noted, in the comparison of job dissatisfactions and attractions. Both myths and information screens serve, in many cases, to assure that a departure will not be interpreted as a departing individual's rejection of his colleagues. This explains the wish to believe that the new position is notably better than the old; for, if it were not, the men remaining in the department would have to ask themselves not "What was better about that job?" but "What was worse about this?" The formal assumption of the superiority of the new job also serves as an ego-saving device for the man who leaves to take an inferior position.

Let us examine this hypothesis to see whether it accounts for some of the phenomena already noted. First, and importantly, it provides an explanation for the support of salary secrecy, even by the working professor who could most benefit by its abolition. If salary information is not available, embarrassing questions about salaries cannot be asked. Salary secrecy lends plausibility to the belief that mobility only occurs toward more attractive positions. The need to defend the department's prestige against invidious comparison also explains the information screens which conceal the circumstances and reasons for departure, the details of the new position elsewhere, and the subsequent careers of former colleagues. The information screens surrounding the activities of seniors, personnel selection procedures, and the criteria for the evaluation of professional merit provide substantial defenses for group morale and the individual ego.

These are only conjectures but, besides the admittedly inconclusive data on dissatisfaction and attraction factors, two other bits of empirical evidence may be brought to bear. A striking feature of the vacancy-and-replacement process is that the notice given by the university to men whom they dismiss is tremendously long compared to the notice given to the university by men who resign. Institutional notice of intention to terminate is often given two or more years in advance, but the modal month for the announcement of resignation from an appointment terminating in June is April. There is one case in the sample of a professor who, one day in June, left an unexpected resignation on his desk after completing the assignment of grades, walked to his car, behind which there was a loaded trailer, and started for the West Coast..Another professor resigned his appointment in August, three weeks before the fall term began.

The best explanation we can give, in view of the fact that the usual open season on candidates is December to April, with many offers made and accepted even earlier, is that resignations must be swift to avoid the tension arising from the inferred rejection. For this reason also, many men who accept offers while away on leave resign by mail and never return to their departments except of a Sunday afternoon to pack their books.

The other bit of empirical evidence on this point concerns the circumstances in which departures take place—in particular the occurrence or absence of a formal farewell. Table 3.4 contains information about the type and frequency of farewell ceremonies for all departures, grouped by rank. The significance of the table may be seen at a glance. Approximately two-thirds of the departing professors received no organized farewell of any kind from their colleagues. Since the department party is a well-established academic ritual everywhere, this omission appears significant. It is especially remarkable that 45 percent of full professors were given no organized farewell—after a median term of fifteen years of service. This lack of ceremony is, in many cases, specifically linked to resentment on the part of the departing man's colleagues:

> "No, there was no formal party as such. I raised the question with him and he said that he'd rather have an informal one with the graduate students than a formal one with the staff. There was hostility on the part of some of his erstwhile colleagues and he knew it and wanted to avoid its open expression."

Table 3.4
Rank of Vacancies by Type of
Farewell Ceremony, in Percent

(N = 147)*

Type of farewell ceremony	Assistant Professor	Associate Professor	Full Professor
None	73	62	45
Informal	20	22	34
Formal	7	16	21
Total	100	100	100

* Excluding involuntary terminations and deaths.

Farewell ceremonies appear to occur with greatest frequency in departments with structures which may be described as highly participant. There is not likely to be a formal farewell in autocratic or factionalized departments unless the departing man happens to be friendly with the autocrat. Take the following, for example.

"Oh good God, no! This department doesn't do things like that. The Chairman is, ah . . . conservative."

It is curious how often contradictory reports were received from members of the department with regard to the send-off given a resigning member. For example:

[From Chairman]:
"No, there was no formal party. Just friends and so forth, a little get-together."

[From Peer]:
"His students gave him a dinner—a very nice dinner. But the faculty did not attend. I don't recall if they were invited; I just don't recall."

When two or more reports of the same departure conflict in this way, the departure itself can usually be explained by schisms in the department.

In summary, resignations from academic departments normally evoke feelings of resentment. It may be possible to leave a department and keep one's friends, but it is difficult to do so and keep one's peers. By the act of leaving, membership in the peer group is given up, and the departing individual is perceived as having rejected his former colleagues. Indeed, too many departures can lower morale until, as in one department, "No one will say goodby when a man retires after fifty years here."

After Departure

The hypothesis that departures are often mutually perceived as rejections receives additional support from an examination of reports concerning the adjustment of men who resigned, in the departments to which they went. In most cases, as previously noted, respondents have little information about their former colleague's satisfaction with his new position, and they assume that he is satisfied with it unless the contrary is definitely known. When this is the case, however, the former colleagues often manifest a distinct attitude of satisfaction in reporting it. There are numerous instances of apparent vindictiveness in respondents' reports of things "which haven't worked out" for their departed colleagues. These are especially noticeable when the man in question has left or has been fired from the position to which he went. They also appear when it is known that he discovered conditions there to be less attractive than he had anticipated. An example of each situation is quoted below.

"I wouldn't know. He praised the department there highly at a meeting when he read a paper, before he knew he wouldn't be reappointed. The chairman there was sitting next to me and he told me at the time, 'We aren't going to re-appoint him.' "

"He's a little unhappy too. Things haven't worked out for him. Same reasons as they didn't here, I suspect. I met the chairman from there last fall and inquired about him, and he was very disappointed. He had presented a paper at a meeting that was very loosely done, very weak."

Collaboration and Isolation

A related question which seems to call for exploration is whether or not collaboration and isolation in the department are related to mobility. In some departments, apparently, the norms favor collaboration between department members; in others, they discourage it. Problems occasionally arise when an individual from a department of the first type, who may be called a "team" man, is hired by a department of the second type. Since he is accustomed to collaborative research, he may feel excluded from the teams he expects to find in operation and suffer some maladjustment in his work habits as a result. When a "lone wolf" researcher from a department of the second type enters a "team" department, he may be accused of antisocial secrecy about his research activities. The two quotations below illustrate these situations.

"During the first year he was always thinking of leaving. He'd come here from a research center and hoped it would be a permanent switch. He didn't receive either the kind of support or physical facilities he'd been promised, and felt a distinct lack of intellectual kinship, emotional and psychological support, congeniality and social response."

"He did start a research program with a man in another department, but not with anyone here. He kept his research secret from all of the faculty of the department until it was printed. It was a great source of trouble. He insisted on intellectual isolation; we had to share equipment. He came to me to borrow equipment and refused to tell what it was to be used for. It was very difficult."

Almost half of the departed men in our sample—42 percent of the assistant professors, 63 percent of the associate professors, and 49 percent of the full professors are said to have been engaged in some collaborative research or writing. It is apparent that collaboration is by far the most common among associate professors—men on their way up.

Our data indicate no apparent differences in the frequency of collaboration between departments which rate high, and those which rate low.

Table 3.5 describes the nine universities sampled by the frequency of collaboration reported for their *departed* faculty members. There seem to be distinct inter-institutional differences, for which our data furnish no explanation.

In fifty-one instances, the respondent reported that he had himself collaborated on writing or research with the former department member. Although the number involved is too small to offer firm conclusions, some interesting tendencies are suggested. It appears that associate professors tend to avoid collaboration with their peers, whereas full professors seek it. In general, we would expect that collaboration with peers would be avoided, since it inevitably involves the participants in each other's reputa-

Table 3.5
Local Variations in the Tendency to Teamwork

Institution	Percent of departed staff members who had collaborated professionally with their departmental colleagues.
University II	63
University VII	61
University III	52
University V	45
University VI	44
University IV	39
University VIII	37
University IX	36
University I	36

tions, whereas the prestige system holds them in competition with one another. A successful collaboration enhances the reputation of each man, but an unsuccessful one imperils the reputations of both.

"Any joint work we had ended the first year. I criticized a paper of his. He would rather publish an error than let a colleague find one in his manuscript."

This dilemma is maximized for the associate professor. Having "arrived" in the academic profession, and having established himself as an independent scholar, he may be expected to be concerned with building his reputation and gaining further promotion and emolument. The same factors operate in the case of the assistant professor, but here they are mitigated by the strong peer group sentiments which prevail at that level. As a man with only one foot on the ladder, the assistant professor is more concerned with getting the other foot on than with the upward climb ahead. He can be expected to have a stronger identification with his peers and less feeling that every colleague is a potential competitor. The familiar phrase "We're all in the same boat" is the password of the peer group. With the peer group as a mutually beneficial and protective society, there is more collaboration between the threatened assistant professors than between the upward-striving, individualistically oriented, associate professors.

The full professor working with a junior collaborator has other problems. For one, increased interaction between individuals of unequal status is bound to lead to a decrease in the status distance between them. For another, the full professor working with a junior man is not only his collaborator but also his judge. The situation is fraught with hazard for both participants. The professor will eventually have to help decide on the promotion or nonpromotion of the junior man. Will their close association be a source of prejudice? From the viewpoint of the junior, a collaboration of this nature is an opportunity either to demonstrate his capabilities or to expose his weaknesses. The possibility of exploitation is always present and, for both, there is the threat of annoying the peers of the other. The junior members of the department may feel that the man in question is getting an inside track by playing up to his senior. The other full professors may feel that their colleague is threatening their collective status by working too closely with an inferior.

We would expect, and we find, that full professors most frequently collaborate with others of their own rank. Collaboration between ranks, when it occurs, takes place between adjacent ranks more frequently than between nonadjacent ranks, since the status distance and the threat of status compromise are less between adjacent ranks.

The level of collaboration reported for men who resigned appears to be somewhat *higher* than the local average. Apparently, isolation is not a major reason for mobility. There is evidence to suggest that the vacancies were better acquainted within their institutions than most of their peers. Only about one-third of the subjects were described as having a narrow range of campus acquaintance, whereas the remainder are said to have been widely acquainted. The departures represent both men on their way up and men on their way down professionally. A possible explanation for the generally wide acquaintance of both groups is that the successful enjoy a high disciplinary prestige, which carries over into social desirability, whereas the unsuccessful compensate for professional inadequacy through social activity—both extreme groups thus exceeding the average sociometric score.

It is interesting to note that isolation, whenever it is mentioned by respondents, is invariably perceived as a problem. This may be because an isolated man within the department is dangerous as long as he is not allied with the peer group.

Discipleship may be regarded as a special case of collaboration. Twelve percent of the men who resigned had students who followed them to another institution. This should probably be counted as a high percentage, since it is extremely difficult for a student, once he is well launched on his doctoral program, to change universities without excessive penalty. The regulations of most graduate schools are rather severe on migrants.

The exact incidence of discipleship in the sample is probably less interesting than the curious attitudes which surround this classic teacher-student relationship. The relationship of master and disciple is honored in principle, as many a scholarly preface attests, but it tends to be somewhat stealthy in practice. Indeed, there is a striking parallel between discipleships and love affairs on the faculty. In both cases, informants who have not participated in such relationships are likely to deny that they ever occur at all. In both cases, the relationship is established unobtrusively, and every effort is made to shield it from general observation, although it may be disclosed with considerable pleasure and pride to close friends of either participant.

The reason for the furtive character of discipleships is very plain. The selection of a single master by a graduate student is almost certain to be interpreted by other members of the faculty as a rejection of themselves, with obvious possibilities of reprisal against either of the parties. The more distinguished a scholar is by comparison with his colleagues, the more freely he may flaunt his disciples. The young or obscure teacher does so at his peril.

For a departing man to take graduate students with him to his new institution is to add injury to insult. In the first place, he discloses the unequivocal existence of a discipleship. In the second place, he deprives the department of movable assets. The following quotation expresses a typical view of the matter.

> "Oh, that wouldn't happen here. This is a team enterprise. A man from here would not let that happen; it would make him feel awkward, discourteous in some way, if he did."

Another "awkward" aspect of the prestige system—especially in the older universities—is the organized, local inner circle of the faculty. This takes various forms. It may be a secret society, a committee for some worthy purpose, an elective club, or a dining arrangement. Its purpose is to confer institutional prestige and, more or less explicitly, to counter the disciplinary prestige, over which the campus elders have no control, with tokens of merit which are closely related to seniority and which have some value in local power politics. The effectiveness of these organizations is hard to gauge accurately. Those who are excluded rationalize their disappointment in the usual phrases:

> "We have no faculty club, just a private club, about fifty members. You get elected, or blackballed, just like a fraternity. I've never applied for membership, but we have three or four men in the department who belong."

These associations tend to disturb the internal cohesion of the faculty in one way while strengthening it in another. They are probably declining in influence as the values of disciplinary prestige become more and more dominant on American campuses—with the ingress of hard-driving, discipline-oriented, young research scholars.

The Outside Offer

One further element in the story of how vacancies occur calls for comment here—namely, the availability of offers from other institutions—since mobility is obviously a function of the opportunity to be mobile. Unfortunately, our statistical evidence on this topic is insufficient, because the relevant questions were not added to the interview schedule until much of the interviewing had been completed. We do have respondents' replies from four of the universities sampled to a query about their own experience with offers from other institutions.

Men at lower prestige levels obtain offers in many ways. They register with placement bureaus, they write to their friends, and they "establish contact" with institutions where they think they would like to teach. On the middle levels of prestige, offers may not be sought, but they do tend to come when a man is known to be unhappy in his position. One respondent's remarks summarize the situation neatly:

"My experience has been definite: when I'm unhappy, I get offers. I get out and prod around, make my availability known, make myself attractive. The guys that I know that are getting offers are the guys that are looking for them. Now this isn't true for the people with real prestige; they get them anyway. But I don't hold with the 'out of the blue' stuff for the others. If a man's happy, he's digging in his lab, not prowling around. Offers always come from or through people that know me. My friends wouldn't suggest me if they knew I was content where I was; they'd feel it was disloyal to me to expose me to temptation."

As this quotation suggests, men at higher prestige levels do not have to let their availability be known. People inquire about them and offers seem to come to them in every mail. The prestige system, however, works in wondrous ways. The men at the very top of a discipline may receive no offers at all because their prestige is too high. It is assumed that their salaries and working conditions are not as good as they should be (for men of such eminence) but are the best which the institution can afford. Most departments will hesitate to make an offer to them, since any offer would be presumably inadequate and, therefore, insulting. If an offer should be received, however, the greatly eminent scholar cannot demand that its terms be met by his own institution, since his prestige requires the assumption that his institution is already doing everything possible for him.

A Theoretical Digression

An organizational status carries with it some degree of power to influence the behavior of others, and it is, therefore, a means for the satisfaction of wants. This is a cumbersome way of saying that an organizational status has value for its holder. The amount of value will depend upon a number of factors. In general, high status, since it carries the possibility of fulfilling more wants, or fulfilling wants more completely than low status in the same organization, will be more valued. Status in an organization in which a member participates heavily will be more highly valued than status in a similar organization in which he participates lightly. The value of a status will also be affected by the nature of the organization—in particular, the ease of entry and departure and the extent to which organizational status is convertible into pleasure, wealth, prestige, or status in other organizations.

Demotion, or loss of status, then, is a decrease in the member's ability to procure satisfactions through the organization, and—on the minimum assumption that some of his behavior is directed toward the achievement of satisfactions and the avoidance of frustration—we may infer not only that demotion will be resisted but that the resistance will be roughly proportionate to the satisfactions which are threatened and the dissatisfaction which will ensue from their loss.

The principle has always been familiar—in one form or another—to administrators attempting to control events in organizations. In the fundamental recurrent problem of how to introduce needed changes into a human group without disrupting it, the principle of status conservation is almost always the key by which the sequence of events leading to a new equilibrium can be discovered.

One final point should be included in this brief discussion. The value of a position to its incumbent is determined not only by his status within the organization but by the prestige of the whole organization in its external environment. An instructorship at a great university is more desirable than a deanship at a local denominational college. Anything, therefore, which tends to lower the prestige of the whole organization constitutes a threat of status loss to each member. This appears to be the basis of the general tendency for members of an organized group to defend it against competing groups of the same type.

Hazards of Interaction

An academic organization, like any other, must maintain a certain minimal level of sociability among its members, but it is possible for a professor, regardless of his own status or prestige, to come into conflict with persons anywhere within the institution. Opponents arise at all levels; note the following, for example.

> "I don't know. I don't think he got along too well with the President of the University."

Similarly, the category of personal reasons for termination includes many interactional nuances. The following quotation refers to a professor who resigned his position for "personal" reasons.

> "I think he was deeply hurt over being relieved as chairman. He resented the choice of a man who was not an acceptable successor to him. This was an element in his leaving. He had administrative talent his successor didn't."

Another situation in which a man's associates are responsible for his mobility is that of rivalry. Many departments are not large enough to contain two strong men, and the one whose prestige is overshadowed or threatened may leave.

> "He was insanely jealous of the success of his departmental colleagues. There was no friction with the senior professor— the age difference protected *him*—but there was with myself and another man when he was acting chairman. The friction went so far that—I don't think this was intentional—he

carried information from staff meetings to the graduate students, distorted so as to build him up a hero and tear the others down."

The characteristics of students may also become a major source of dissatisfaction. Consider the following, for example:

"He was extremely critical of the mediocrity of a great many of his students. He was heartily disliked by some—many—students, and worshiped by some others. He always had a coterie of 7 to 10 graduate students around him. He had no sympathy with mediocrity, never understood that a great many of the people of the world are mediocre in intelligence."

One cause of dissatisfaction which is difficult to classify is the "historical accident." Often concealed under some other label, historical accidents account for a small but significant number of terminations. The category is best defined by illustration.

"For a long time before he became a professor, he was irked by the slowness of promotion. And it was slow for the same reason that has been true in many large departments since the war. There have to be so many teachers, primarily teachers of service courses, although of course they do not think of themselves in that category. We had a special problem here when we inaugurated the 'up or out' promotion system. What happened was that a lot of men who had been here a long time and weren't on the 'up or out' list because they'd been appointed before it took effect, asked to have themselves put on it so they could either force their promotions or get out. This all happened at the time right after the war when teachers were impossible to get. It resulted in the promotion of men to permanent tenure that we wouldn't normally have promoted. So the ranks of associate professors have become very crowded. It's still with us. Our attitude now is that if the younger ones are better, they'll just have to be promoted over the older ones that aren't so good."

It seems to be generally the case that a man's peers are more aware of his dissatisfactions than his superiors, as illustrated by the quotations below. The first is by the chairman of the department, the second by one of the man's peers. Note the cataloguing of the specific complaints in the latter.

"Well, I don't think so. The only unsatisfactory thing was the uncertainty as to whether he would be promoted or not."

"Yes: uncertainty about future permanence, a certain dissatisfaction with other members of the staff professionally, a lack of graduate students to do research under him. That's both a departmental problem and a rather acute personal one, in this case."

The typical discrepancies between the responses of chairmen and peers in this section of the interview can best be explained by reference to the distribution of authority in the academic status system. A professor will generally complain to his chairman only about matters which are beyond the latter's control, for to complain about a matter within the chairman's scope is to challenge his authority. Thus complaints about the chairman will be made to peers, one of whom will carry the tale to the chairman. In this way the status of the peer is enhanced, since the act of making the complaint to him implies that he can do something about it. The peer, in turn, is able to confront the chairman because the complaint is not his own. As an intermediary, he is not challenging the chairman's authority and will not fear retaliation.

It is this interplay of statuses which best explains why each status level is more friendly toward the next lower adjacent level than toward lower nonadjacent levels. Thus, the dean feels closer to the chairman than to other professors, and the president feels closer to the dean than to chairmen; the situation being always structured in such a way that the chairman carries the complaints of other professors to the dean, and the dean carries the complaints of chairmen to the president. Since status considerations do not permit the complainer to present the criticism as his own, he must play the role of sympathetic intermediary. In effect, he identifies himself with the higher adjacent status level, reassuring his superior of identification with *him* and not with the rabble he is forced, by the nature of his position, to represent.

An interesting demonstration of the complexity of the status system is the fact that an unsuccessful candidate for a position may acquire, by his unsuccessful candidacy, some measure of the status which that position commands. In any event he is likely to acquire a vested right to be recommended again.

"We sent in a list of seven. The President wouldn't have it; he felt they weren't worth it. We kept sending in their names, because once you have, you've got to try again" [italics added].

Table 3.6 describes the distribution of reports of dissatisfaction according to department rating. As might be

Table 3.6
Dissatisfaction Before Departure
by Department Rating, in Percent

Reported dissatisfied	High-rated Department	Low-rated Department
No	51	35
Yes	49	65

expected, more men leaving poorer departments are reported to have been discontented than men leaving better departments. Tables 3.7 and 3.8 describe the distribution

Table 3.7
Dissatisfaction Before Departure
by Rank of Vacancy, in Percent

Reported dissatisfied	Assistant Professor	Associate Professor	Full Professor
No	52	33	45
Yes	48	67	55

of reports of dissatisfaction according to rank and departure categories. The gross amount of reported dissatisfaction is striking.

In summary, these findings lend support to the view that the "push" of academic migration is stronger than the "pull." The majority of vacancies cannot be attributed to the lure of opportunities elsewhere but to dissatisfaction—either the failure of the incumbent to please his associates or their failure to please him, or both. These dissatisfactions can be most economically explained by reference to the system of disciplinary prestige.

Table 3.8
Dissatisfaction Before Departure
by Type of Departure, in Percent

Reported dissatisfied	Resigned	Died	Retired
No	44	53	59
Yes	56	47	41

Chapter 4

HOW
Performance
IS
Evaluated

In any discussion of contemporary standards for the evaluation of academic men, the first, and major, point to be made is that there is a great deal of confusion in American universities with regard to the role of the professor in his institution and profession. As Logan Wilson pointed out some years ago,

> "In view of the vague and conflicting criteria by which his work is judged, he is uncertain in the allocation of his energies. He knows that he is a competitor, but often is not clear regarding the terms of the competition." [1]

The foremost element in this confusion is uncertainty about the relative importance accorded to the two fundamental academic activities: teaching and research. The problem of the professor who is not research-minded is a formidable one. Basically, he is playing against time, since he has only a limited number of years in which to meet the requirements for tenure and to be reasonably assured of a

---

[1] *Op. cit.*, p. 62.

future in his chosen profession. If he is able to publish at all, however, he is not impossibly handicapped, since the actual number of publications necessary to meet tenure requirements at most universities is not large. Once having a tenure appointment, he may drop all serious effort (although not all pretense) at research and still hope to receive further promotion and emolument for other services rendered to the university.

"Publish or Perish"

For most members of the profession, the real strain in the academic role arises from the fact that they are, in essence, paid to do one job, whereas the worth of their services is evaluated on the basis of how well they do another. The work assignment, for which the vast majority of professors are paid, is that of teaching. There are a few —a very few—who are supported by full- or part-time regular research appointments, but their number is insignificant compared to the vast majority who are hired to teach, and in whose contracts no specification of research duties is made. Most professors contract to perform teaching services for their universities and are hired to perform those services. When they are evaluated, however, either as candidates for a vacant position, or as candidates for promotion, the evaluation is made principally in terms of their research contributions to their disciplines. The following quotation is an interesting case in point; note the after-effects on the peers.

> "Among other things, he coached the student group. He got canned by an *ad hoc* committee which split 4 to 3 in his favor, but it was decided to can him on the basis of the split. Some of us feel that this was a case of real campus politics.

It may have been honest and it may not, but it was clear that his really tremendous work with this student group hadn't been weighted at all in the consideration of his promotion. He did a really tremendous job. It caused the rest of us to decide that if this kind of activity was not what was honored —and he'd led them to several national recognitions—then we'd do what was honored—namely, sitting in the library and writing weighty papers, and let their goddamned student group go to hell, which it has."

It is neither an overgeneralization nor an oversimplification to state that in the faculties of major universities in the United States today, the evaluation of performance is based almost exclusively on publication of scholarly books or articles in professional journals as evidence of research activity. Out of 371 responses to the question, "Do you think he has reached the peak of his productivity as yet?" 122 respondents define "productivity" unmistakably as research, or publication of research; only 14 refer either directly or indirectly to the teaching of students; and 11 of these 14 qualify the importance of teaching in some way. The other 235 responses are so worded that it is impossible to state what criteria are being used for productivity. Throughout the interviews, however, departures from the publication formula for productivity are rare indeed. The explicit definition of publication as the criterion of productivity is very common. In addition, respondents often specifically exclude from consideration other activities, such as teaching, administration, creative artistry, public service, or internal service to the university.

"Yes, he's getting involved with administration there, and that's the kiss of death for any research."

"It's my opinion that he will never be a productive scholar. He reads very widely and will be content to be a teacher and

perhaps do a little creative writing—he used to write poetry
—but he will never be a producing scholar."

"She hasn't been in positions where productivity was demanded or even permitted. She's always been a practicing
clinician; in her current job there's no time for research. I
would say that if this goes on, her peak has been reached."

"In his new job, he's going to be led into more superficial
kinds of writing—for popular consumption—well, summaries
for businessmen."

It has been suggested that the recent emphasis on
team research in the social and physical sciences may be, in
part, a protective device for the non-research-minded professor and for his counterpart who can do research but
finds it difficult to put his results in publishable form.
There is some evidence, of an admittedly speculative character, to support this contention. It appears that research
teams are usually composed of one strong research worker,
or "idea man," and a number of less brilliant colleagues
working more or less under his direction. It is also commonly alleged that team research is somehow identified
with qualitatively inferior work. These are only assertions,
however, and there are many instances of brilliant results
attributable to teams, and of research situations (*e.g.* high-
energy nuclear physics) which require team effort. Certainly
a team *may* provide the protection of joint publication for
a man who would not otherwise see his name in print.
Until quite recently, no such recourse was available, but,
on the other hand, teaching had greater importance.

"He came here as a young man, and at the time the head
of the department forbade research—said that it destroyed a
man's capacity to teach."

It is interesting, after this echo of an older ethic, to realize that the criterion of publication is rationalized today by the argument that research activity is essential to effective teaching. Formerly, it was possible to make a career either in the university *or* in the discipline, and the man who chose a local career sustained himself through service to the institution and personal relationships in the faculty. The campus elder statesman is still a familiar figure on American university campuses, but it would seem that, as the present elders retire, there will not be many of a younger generation to take their places.

Today, a scholar's orientation to his institution is apt to disorient him to his discipline and to affect his professional prestige unfavorably. Conversely, an orientation to his discipline will disorient him to his institution, which he will regard as a temporary shelter where he can pursue his career as a member of the discipline. And he will be, as a matter of course, considerably more mobile than his institutionally oriented colleagues. In a handful of great universities, where many of the departments believed to be the best in their fields are found, a merger of orientations is possible. There a man may simultaneously serve an institution and a discipline and identify with both. But tensions exist between the two orientations everywhere. It is worthy of note that the publication requirements in the highest ranking departments are the most rigid, so that the men they select have already met the requirements imposed by the discipline.

Several respondents referred to the "guild aspect" of certain disciplines—especially mathematics and physics. Their comments seem to assert that, in these fields at least, for the successful professor the institutional orientation has entirely disappeared.

The Career Curve

We note in the responses of informants that peaks are always found, or assumed, in the academic career. It is a familiar fact that in different occupations careers tend to peak at different ages. This occurs within the academic profession as well, with considerable variation from one discipline to another. The extremes may be represented by history, a field in which men in their late forties are often referred to as "young," and by mathematics, where men are frequently said to have "burned out" (*i.e.*, completed their contributive careers) in their early thirties.

> "I'd say he reached his mathematical peak years ago. There are damned few people that do any thinking after they're forty. I'm not competent to judge any other kind of peak. I'm no intellectual—neither was he."

There are many questions of superannuation which affect the contemporary academic labor market. A common theme is the dissatisfaction of younger men with the productivity of their elders. The following quotations illustrate the tone of a number of such responses.

> "Yes, his leaving meant that there are no longer any non-productive full professors. He had little sympathy for graduate work and research."

> "He believed that conviviality and sociability were the prime qualities for a professor. We had parties twice a month, played golf, etc., all the time. We also had a lousy department. There have been some fundamental changes around here."

It is impossible to say just how much of the reported superannuation is due to a real decrease in research potential and how much to the encounter between the institutional orientation of the older men and the disciplinary orientation of the younger (with its increased stress on publication). It has been remarked before that prestige is, in part, a function of mobility or potential mobility, and that an older man's potential mobility is low.

An academic man's career is normally only half over at the age of fifty. Most academic men enter the labor market today at about thirty, upon receipt of the Ph.D., and since the usual age of compulsory retirement is about seventy, a man of fifty can still look forward to as many working years as lie behind him. Yet, unless he is widely known, his mobility after fifty is very, very limited. We can see two reasons for this. The first is that the retirement plans in effect at most institutions require a fairly long term of service for sizable benefits to accrue; the second is that evaluation by the criterion of research productivity tends to fix the market value of a man in proportion to the volume of future research expected from him. (We would expect, therefore, that the mobility potential of a middle-aged historian would be higher than that of a mathematician of the same age. The data of the study do not permit a test of this expectation.)

Labels and Markings

In attempting to describe the ways in which scholars may be categorized by their colleagues, we need to make certain very general distinctions. In the humanities, schools of thought are defined with considerable subjectivity, and a description is often most informative for what it says about the perspective of the describer.

"Cerebral, as opposed to visceral or emotional. He knew why he did what he did . . . it always made sense. That's the kind of man we need, so he can explain it to students."

Of those disciplines covered in the study, evaluation in English is probably the most complex because it is the most thoroughly subjective. The only consensus in reports from English departments is on the importance of the "New Criticism," but even here there is disagreement within departments on whether a departed member was or was not one of the New Critics. In literature and languages, specialists are typically categorized by historical era, such as "sixteenth century." Art, surprisingly, displays more system.

> "In general he was an abstract expressionist. More specifically, abstract impressionism. The difference is really not great."

In the natural sciences, the question "Is there any particular professional viewpoint with which he is identified?" tended to be resented by the respondents, apparently because the physical scientist thinks of "viewpoints" as being polemical and believes that science has outgrown them. Note the unanimity in the following set of responses from one university's physics department.

> "I'm not aware of different viewpoints or schools in physics."

> "There are no schools in physics."

> "No, I don't. I never thought of physicists as belonging to schools."

> "That's not a meaningful question in science."

Among the natural sciences, we judge, on the basis of reports, that categorization is simplest in physics, where, within some specialties, there is a virtual interchangability of human parts. Chemistry does not seem to have achieved this degree of simplicity but exhibits a highly ramified division of labor with substantial agreement on what the subdivisions of the discipline are.

> "I don't quite understand [that question]. In chemistry he'd be classified as an inorganic physical chemist."

About the social sciences it is almost impossible to generalize. They seem to be in a transitional stage between the complex subjectivity of the humanities and the fragmentary objectivity of the natural sciences. Some distinction can be drawn, however, among the various disciplines. In economics, classification is often made on political grounds—a distinction shared, oddly, with departments of Eastern European language, literature, and culture. Note the political basis of the categories in the quotations below:

> "He was generally orthodox, rather on the conservative side."

> "Since this [Slavic] is a particularly delicate field, the man has to be able to get along with all sorts of people. There is a question of temperament which is not invoved in any other area of history. There are national antagonisms, there's sensitivity about the subdivisions of the Slavic field, and there are also class and status differentiations. Many of these people are exiles, and former aristocrats find it hard to get along with someone from the ghetto."

Geography enjoys the distinction among the social sciences of having *two* categories for each practitioner, one methodological and the other regional.

> "He was a systematic geographer with a regional approach, and represented a fusion of schools. He helped develop the concept of the functional organization of regions."

> "We needed someone in cartography and Southeast Asia."

Once the happy hunting ground of schools and viewpoints, psychology has today resolved most of its conflicts and classifications into a single dichotomy of pure (experimental) and applied (clinical) science.

"He was a pure experimentalist."

Sociology, like psychology, has left the earlier and more subjective strife behind, and classification is generally made on the basis of operating skills, with the problem in the hiring process of matching the methods of the candidate with those prevailing in the hiring department. Note the case below of a man with a proficient combination of methods, which is seen as enhancing his potential value.

"He represented a combination of theory and empirical work, a very desirable person for that reason, one of the few people to combine theory and research. In that generation, the Davis-Merton generation, everyone is Parsonian."

To summarize for all the areas, we may say that, in general, a scholar may be classified either by the content or by the method of his studies but that most disciplines emphasize one of these over the other. The differences of viewpoint which matter, and which influence the outcome of candidacies, are directed to content or method, depending on the prevailing emphasis of the discipline.

To give some examples from social science, it is possible for liberal and conservative economists, men with different viewpoints on the *content* of their field, to be in substantial agreement on its *method*. Sociology, on the other hand, makes a common distinction between empiricists and theorists. These might be said to be in substantial agreement on the *content* of their field but hold different viewpoints on *method*.

It is possible, in most disciplines, to specialize in either content or method, with varying degrees of specialization and of doctrinal bias. The most notable characteristic of the professional viewpoint is that it tends to exclude from consideration the result obtained by men with other viewpoints. Thus, a liberal economist may use almost the same methods as his conservative counterpart without seeing any usefulness in the findings of the conservative's investigations. The statistically minded sociologist, similarly, has no quarrel with the social theorist about the content of what they are both studying but sees little utility for himself in the results obtained by the other. These differences have great force when adherents of one viewpoint find themselves in the position of having to evaluate the adherents of another:

> "He was a protégé of mine. After he'd gotten the degree, he and I collaborated on a number of articles in the field of education. We propounded in one monograph an unorthodox theory which was a violent attack on the traditional concepts and philosophies of Progressive Education. Now when his review committee was made up, there was a man from the college of education on it and another from one of their satellite departments. I am convinced, absolutely convinced, that the unorthodox character of this article lost him his job. His heretical opinions. You know how these people can get when their pet dogmas are attacked."

Evaluation of a man is always a function of (1) his specialty and (2) the viewpoint of the evaluator. Identifications of a colleague's specialty—either in content or in method—tend to be fairly straightforward. The evaluation of its importance, however, tends to be confused and emotional. Note, for example, the following quotation from two respondents in a mathematics department, where the identification of the specialty is quite simple, but where evident differences of viewpoint intervene in the evaluation.

> "He was a member of the early American school of topology. By early, I mean 1920-1930. That particular school has gone out of style."

> "In branch, he was a topologist. It is now flourishing, particularly in America, and is being continued in our department, of course, by others."

The evaluation of candidates in those disciplines in which men are hired by specialty is relatively simple, but there is considerable mobility because men are so easily replaced, and replacements are so readily identifiable, that it is not difficult for any individual to become surplus. In fields in which there are strong conflicts of viewpoint, hiring and evaluation are slow and difficult because agreement about the merits, or even about the characteristics, of a candidate cannot easily be achieved. Evaluation is necessarily uncertain in such a field, since it depends upon the viewpoint of the evaluator. The following is an excellent case in point.

> "We asked for some letters on him, and among them was one from a prominent man which was very unfavorable to him in terms of his 'school.' I didn't neutralize it sufficiently, I guess, although I'd thought it would be obvious to the committee what the difference was. They wouldn't hire him."

It is often extremely difficult to distinguish in respondents' reports between classifications of men based on their specialties and those based on their viewpoints. Perhaps the best example, from a female informant, was the following.

> "His wife was a quarrelsome, gossipy, shallow, woman. He was interested in Milton."

One sure mark of the *organized* viewpoint, however, is the suffix "-ian" attached to a proper name—Lewinian, Parsonian, Boasian. This term marks the viewpoint of a particular scholar whose disciples have become a faction in the discipline. It always implies personal contact with others of the same persuasion and certain kinds of "kin rights," or claims for professional assistance. The organized viewpoint, thus, rests partly on intellectual conviction, and partly on disciplinary politics. It serves the function for its adherents of automatically identifying alignments of friends, enemies, and possible allies in any academic situation. Note some of these elements here.

> "He was very much a follower of Franz Boas—a much closer and more literal follower than many. Definitely Boasian, very consciously so—he sought the identification. He saw anthropology as a professional field rather than as a subject of value in a liberal arts curriculum as a service course. That's a little different than the way most people view it. He never opened his courses to freshmen and rather discouraged majoring in anthropology, etc."

One final remark on professional evaluation is perhaps in order. The data leave us with a strong impression, which we would find difficult to demonstrate statistically, that although the scholar's judgment of his colleagues is often blind and biased, and occasionally downright crazy, it *is* professional. Men are not judged by their tempers or their table manners, unless either of these is unspeakably bad. The judgment made is based on performance and is as equitable as conflicts of viewpoint permit. Although the judge may not be impartial, he does seem to confine his judgment to what is relevant—and to succeed remarkably well in keeping nonprofessional factors out of his consideration.

Chapter 5

THE
Strategy
OF THE
Department

We have noted at several points that their former colleagues attribute to departed men a considerable amount
of general dissatisfaction. It might also be inferred from
the typical unenthusiastic farewell and from the under-
statement of the vacancy's impact that there is a considerable amount of departmental dissatisfaction with the departed men. In some cases, this dissatisfaction takes the
form of hostility and resentment toward them. It is not surprising, then, for us to discover that, when a man receives
an offer from another university, the effort made to hold
him where he is seldom consists of anything more than a
matching of the financial offer from the outside institution, and in many cases not even this. Table 5.1 describes
167 terminations and the attempts made by the departments in which they occurred to retain the men who left.
The significance of the table lies in the fact that in 61 percent of the cases, the chairman of the department knew of
no effort to prevent the resignation.

Table 5.1

Rank of Vacancy by Effort to

Prevent Vacancy, in Percent

(N = 167 Resignations)

Effort to prevent vacancy	Assistant Professor	Associate Professor	Full Professor	Total Sample
Definitely none	31	12	5	21
Probably none	41	34	45	40
Probably some	25	38	38	31
Definitely some	3	16	12	8
	100	100	100	100

The fact that universities do not, in many cases, make any effort to retain staff who have received offers from other institutions contradicts a good deal of academic folklore and demands explanation. Why is this so?

Offers and Counter-offers

In many instances, the department perceives the outside offer as the resolution for a difficult situation. Not infrequently the man who receives such an offer is one whom the department would like to be rid of—either because he is unpopular with his colleagues or because they are unpopular with him. If a department makes an effort to retain a dissatisfied member, it runs the risk of having its offer refused and thus making his rejection of them explicit. The quotation below is an illustration of a common rationalization for not counter-bidding in such a situation.

> "Well, I think everyone wanted him to stay, but as far as I know I think he simply decided he was leaving and that was it."

Another facet of departmental prestige-sensitivity is the very common reluctance to bid openly against stiff competition and thus run the risk of being publicly outbid by another university. For this reason, universities with a reputation for "getting the men they go after" have an advantageous position in the labor market.

> "We went to a salary offer of $7000 for him. He was a good man, but he went to Harvard. It was straight competition. We were playing against the Big League in trying to keep him, and we didn't have the stuff to do it with."

When a university does make an attempt to retain a man who has received an outside offer (except in the relatively rare case of a man of great eminence), the effort is usually minimal. It may normally be expected to occur under one of the three following conditions.

The counter-offer may be an effort to protect the local prestige of the individual involved. A university which fails to meet an offer is almost sure to lose the faculty member, even to an inferior position, once he has brought the matter officially to attention and thereby signified his willingness to leave if the offer is not met. A minimal amount of encouragement or a nominal salary increase may be offered—even to a man of whom the department would as soon be quit—in order to avoid the open expression of hostility which a failure to make any move to retain him would suggest. The parting is thus smoothed for both parties.

The second condition under which a counter-offer may be made (famous scholars again excepted) is that hiring a replacement is impossible or inconvenient. It must be remembered that in many universities the hiring process is so involved, so tedious, and so cumbersome, that it may easily be regarded as the penalty for the occurrence of a vacancy. If the disputed individual is one to whom the department members are largely indifferent, it may seem worth the effort to retain him simply to avoid the greater effort of replacing him.

A counter-offer is sometimes made to a professor after he receives an outside offer which was arranged for that very purpose. It is a full-scale academic myth, which was quoted to the investigators many times, that the only way to get a promotion in X or Y University is to receive an offer from somewhere else. In reality, the Ceremonial Bluff, as it may be called, is fairly rare. (We distinguish this from the case of a man's receiving a bona fide offer from another university in which he is genuinely interested, although the empirical results are frequently identical.) It can sometimes be used only once per university, or perhaps once per rank, although there are exceptions, of course. Several instances were reported of men whose previous success with the Ceremonial Bluff emboldened them to repeat it only to find it called. And it cannot be attempted safely with just any offer. A bid from an obviously inferior institution tips the player's hand, sometimes with the consequence of a one-way trip to academic Siberia.

There seems to be, in the universities studied, a distinct administrative reaction against attempts to force the institutional hand. The Ceremonial Bluff may be permitted once in order to validate a man's prestige in the department or the college. It may, in fact, be encouraged by the departmental administration for this purpose. The academic man normally has his prestige validated in his department and institution by his peers, who refer to his work with respect and indicate to the outside world in other ways that he is worthy of his position. A man without a peer group may be encouraged by his chairman to solicit an offer or two in order that the chairman may demonstrate to higher authority that he is earning his keep. It is most unusual, however, for a university to allow an individual to continue to raise his salary in this manner, and many deans keep a no-bidding policy in reserve for such occasions. The quotation below, referring to a case of Ceremonial Bluffing which resulted in a resignation, shows this tactic in action:

> "Yes [we tried to keep him]; we went to the Dean to see if we couldn't match their salary. We couldn't. I think the Dean has a policy of not trying to simply outbid another institution. The Dean said to let him go."

Some departments respond to all outside offers with the suspicion that the recipient is soliciting them, and even under the best conditions counter-offers do not always develop as expected.

> "We talked about it with him. We couldn't meet the salary, and it was clear that he wasn't interested in staying on if we didn't. We didn't think that it was worth meeting it. I guess you'd say that the offer came, he liked it, and we said, 'Bye, sorry you're leaving.' "

The Matter of Salary

Table 5.2 compares the average salaries and the frequency of salary complaints in the universities in our sample, grouped into high-salary and low-salary institutions for each rank.

A quick glance at Table 5.2 will show that salary is not a major cause of dissatisfaction for full professors, regardless of the relative positon of their universities in the institutional salary order. Perhaps more surprising is the fact that salary grievances are reported less frequently in the low-salary universities, especially by the low-salary assistant professors, with average earnings of only $4647.

The greater salary dissatisfaction of full and assistant professors at the high-salary universities lends further support to the conclusion that faculty mobility is not a simple function of salary differentials.

Table 5.2

Salary Dissatisfaction of Vacancies
by Institution and Rank*

	FOUR UNIVERSITIES WITH LOWEST SALARIES		FOUR UNIVERSITIES WITH HIGHEST SALARIES	
Vacancy Rank	*Mean Salary*	*% Dissatisfied*	*Mean Salary*	*% Dissatisfied*
Assistant Professor	$4647	11	$5588	33
Associate Professor	$5523	33	$7045	27
Full Professor	$7530	4	$10,337	8

* The table was derived as follows: reported salaries of vacancies were averaged by rank for each university. Institutions were then rank-ordered, the median case removed for each of the three ranks, and the eight remaining institutional cases grouped into high-salary and low-salary categories for each academic rank. The average salary by rank for these two categories was then computed. Reported salary ranges and medians by rank were:

	Assistant Professor	*Associate Professor*	*Full Professor*
Range	$4250-5675	$5235-7600	$5973-11,231
Median	$5142	$6500	$8967

The Impact of Departure

Table 5.3, indicating the impact of the vacancy on the department, supports the hypothesis that departure is perceived as rejection. Important consequences are admitted in only 11 percent of the cases, of which more than half are voluntary departures or departures by death or retirement. If resignations are interpreted as rejections, it is a plausible inference that the members of the department are reluctant to acknowledge the full effect of departures in that category. In the case of death or retirement, however, where no rejection can be attributed, it involves no self-depreciation to admit a loss. It is also true that death and retirement are most apt to carry off full professors, whose departures may be expected to have the most impact on a department; but it is instructive to note that the number of de-

Table 5.3

Rank of Vacancy by Reported Impact in Department

	RESIGNED					TOTAL	
Reported Impact	*Asst. Pro-fessor*	*Assoc. Pro-fessor*	*Full Pro-fessor*	DIED	RE-TIRED	*Number*	%
Definitely none	6	—	—	1	1	8	4
Practically none	72	16	13	8	17	126	58
Some	11	10	12	6	10	49	23
Severe	3	4	4	6	6	23	11
No response	4	1	1	—	1	7	3
Uncodable	—	1	1	—	—	2	1
Total	96	32	31	21	35	215	
Percent	45	15	14	10	16		100

partures admitted to have had an impact, but not due to death or retirement, are also in order of rank, being, respectively 15, 45, and 55 percent. The significance of Table 5.3 is that impact is admitted for only about one-third of the departures taking place. Impact is positively related to academic rank.

The questions about the impact of departures elicit a number of standard responses. Most prevalent of these is the assertion that "no man is indispensable," which usually implies that the department was unaffected in its functions. We shall let our informants speak for themselves in illustration of this theme.

> "If you have a man four years, this causes some upset. No man is irreplaceable, so yes—and no—to the question of impact. The department hasn't gone to hell, or what-have-you. If I were to quit, there'd be two months of confusion and then things would go on as well as before, maybe better."

Another frequent theme is the "change of emphasis"; it meant the shift in emphasis from one dominant viewpoint to another, as shown by comments such as this:

> "No, it didn't alter our formal offering a bit; he didn't do any graduate teaching. However, I think that its major impact was a signal to some of the other people here that there was a new order in the saddle—it indicated the onset of pressures."

Next most common is what might be called the "opened door" theme: "His departure has made it possible for us to. . . ."

> "It tended to further the deterioration of the department and precipitated another resignation that burst the boil, and now everyone is well and happy again, and we are really beginning to go to town."

Common in the sciences is the "replaceable parts" theme, usually expressed by something like the following (not an actual quotation): "He was a theoretical multidimensional geobarbanalyst. They're dirt cheap; we got another." Even in disciplines in which this theme appears, however, the hiring process continues to be dominated by other assumptions. The care with which men are selected in most departments, the rigors of the evaluation process, the sometimes unbelievably complicated apparatus devised for the discovery of candidates—all imply that the men to be hired are so nearly unique as to be virtually irreplaceable. That nothing could be further from the truth, especially in the case of junior appointments, is demonstrated both by Table 5.3 and by the rapidity with which, in most departments, the newly hired hand is assimilated.

On the other hand, in a few of the departments studied, the junior faculty is not identified with the department by the senior professors. A case in point is the following:

> "A department like this usually functions by having a core, a large body of permanent members. Then the junior positions are given aspirants, not with the expectation that they will stay, but with a chance to earn a reputation, which will get them a permanent job elsewhere. It is no great disappointment to them or anyone else if they leave."

This attitude, even when rationalized in terms of the professional welfare of the juniors, presents a strange contrast to the attitudes exhibited in the recruiting process. The only explanation we can make for this inconsistency is that it seems to appear in departments with traditionally high mobility. Perhaps the permanent members of this type of department wish to avoid involvement with temporary appointees who are not likely to remain.

The Department's Prestige

Table 5.4 describes the relationship between the chair-

Table 5.4

Rank of Vacancies by

Department Rating, in Percent

(N = 157 departments)

	DEPARTMENT RATING		
Vacancy rank	*Among the first five*	*Better than average*	*Average or worse*
Assistant Professor	39	49	50
Associate Professor	21	22	33
Full Professor	40	29	17
Total	100	100	100

man's rating of his department's prestige in its discipline and the distribution of mobility by ranks. It shows a clearly significant association between the standing of the department, as rated by its chairman, and the relative mobility of senior, as compared to junior, staff members. It may at first seem surprising that the better departments show a higher rate of mobility among full professors, but this is consistent with our other evidence concerning the greater disciplinary orientation which prevails in such departments.

Table 5.5 includes hypothetical as well as empirical data. A tendency for departments to be overrated by their members—the Aggrandizement Effect—has already been noted. It is arithmetically implausible for 37 percent of the departments sampled to be "among the first five in the country" in their disciplines. The table estimates the extent of the Aggrandizement Effect.

Many problems of academic recruiting arise from this phenomenon. Professors do not, in general, overrate departments other than their own. Since they are unrealistic in rating their own department but realistic in their evaluation of others, it comes about that, whenever a department rates itself against another from which it hires staff, or which hires staff from it, it is involved' in a comparison which is partly false. This is another reason why departments hesitate to engage in competitive bidding. To do so is to expose their self-ratings to an objective test. We have a number of instances, for example, of two-man departments whose chairman rated the department "better than

Table 5.5
Expected and Actual Department Ratings,
in Percent*

(N = 157 departments)

	Among the first five	Better than average	Average	Poorer than average	Total
Expected	12.5	12.5	50.0	25.0	100.0
Actual	50.7	35.6	9.6	4.1	100.0

* The expected percentages were computed on the assumption that all of the first five departments in all fields would be found in the forty universities which are members of the A. A. U., giving any department chosen at random within our sample a ⅛ (12.5%) probability of falling in the first five, that the "better than average" category is as populous as the "among the first five" category, and that deviations below the average are as numerous as the deviations above the average. These assumptions tend to be conservative in that distributions based on alternative assumptions show even sharper discrepancies between actual and expected percentages.

average for major institutions." It seems doubtful that a self-image of this nature could be preserved if the department were to engage in competitive bidding for candidates or attempt to retain a member who had received an attractive offer from another university.

Another consequence of the Aggrandizement Effect is the tendency of men in great departments to disparage other departments in their disciplines. Those who *really* belong "among the first five" tend to see themselves as flatly *first*. It is notable that, when asked to explain the success of one of the others in "luring" a staff member away from them, they tend to cite personal factors and very seldom admit the attractiveness of the competing department.

The Aggrandizement Effect is by no means unique to academic departments. It appears to be a general characteristic of sets of intercommunicating similarly structured organizations. The senior author, in a study of fifty-five sets of six organizations of varied types [1] found that raters overestimated the prestige of their own organization eight times as frequently as they underestimated it, and that net overestimation of the prestige of the raters' own organizations could be discerned in every one of the sets. However, the extent of the Aggrandizement Effect was less for almost all these systems, which were confined to a single locality, than for the widely dispersed academic departments.

[1] Fraternities, sororities, teen-age clubs, Protestant churches, Catholic parishes, public high schools, private colleges, dance studios, nursing schools, hospital services, chain hamburger stands, savings and loan associations, pest-control firms, community centers, country clubs, dress shops, advertising agencies, Campfire Girl groups, branch Y.M.C.A.'s, photographic studios, Young Judea clubs, banks, chain supermarkets, printing firms, employment agencies, architectural firms, insurance agencies, foreign-student clubs, Skid Row missions, trucking firms, department stores, religious youth organizations, social science departments.

The Grapevine

Another academic myth concerns a "grapevine" which keeps departments well informed about candidates, and candidates well-informed about vacancies. A communications grapevine typically develops when persons who are not formally required to communicate have reciprocal utilities for one another's information. Wherever a good grapevine is found, as among professional musicians, it is maintained because its participants have something to gain from it and nothing to lose. This is not the case in the academic profession, where the grapevine is incomplete and works rather badly. Let us examine it in the light of the hiring process.

From a chairman's point of view, an ideal grapevine would circulate the characteristics and availability of *all* candidates except those in his own department. From a candidate's standpoint, the ideal grapevine would circulate full information about all positions except those to which he is specifically recommended. A chairman, of course, would prefer to withhold the negative features of the positions he was trying to fill, and a candidate would prefer to conceal the flaws in his own record.

Thus, efficient communication between departments is not consistently prized. Much of the communication which does occur represents not the passage but the blockage of information. The message transmitted will always depend, to some degree, on the relative prestige of sender and receiver. Take the departmental feud as an example. As a subject of communication, it may either be exposed—in order to obtain outside support for the faction to which the exposer belongs—or concealed—in order to maintain departmental prestige. Any given communicator may select either alternative, depending on the identity of his listener. To a man of high standing in the discipline, the communicator may reveal all the details in an effort to align the prestigious individual with his faction. The great influence of his listener makes maintenance of departmental prestige less important to the communicator than the protection of their pair relationship. If, on the other hand, the listener is of low prestige, it is likely that nothing about the feud will be communicated, and the appearance of group solidarity will be carefully maintained.

Prestige Exchanges

It would appear that the ability of great departments to hold staff is no better than that of mediocre departments. This can be explained by the prestige system of the discipline. The higher the rank of the department in the disciplinary prestige system, the more it serves its individual members by conferring a derivative reputation on them. This reputation tends to make them more desirable to other universities, more independent of their own, and more inclined to mobility. It should be mentioned in passing that members of high-prestige departments tend to be mobile in more than one sense. The faculty of great departments are generally inveterate travelers, shuttling from Teheran to Texas and from one Cambridge to the other on scholarly errands which—by convention—do not need to be fully explained.

A further point which must be emphasized in any discussion of departmental prestige is that the higher the prestige of a department, the greater will be the tendency for its members to be oriented to the discipline rather than to the university. The important fact about what men in the major league regard as second-rate institutions is that men earn their academic reputations *within* these institutions. This fact also accounts, in part, for the relatively lower faculty mobility in institutions of lower prestige. Since prestige-gaining activities at these universities and colleges are not disciplinary but institutional, they discourage mobility by rewarding effort in a nontransferrable currency and for nonmobility producing activities. The junior man who secures tenure in a department of high prestige is not irrevocably committed to that university or that department; in fact, the promotion probably lessens his commitment. An assistant professor at a lesser institution will struggle just as hard for tenure, but his potential mobility will be decreased by its attainment.

We have seen that in the high-prestige institutions men are hired on an estimate of how much research they are likely to do. When their tenure is decided, direct utility to the university hardly enters as a factor in the decision to keep them. The measurement of their worth is haunted by quite another problem—their usefulness in *future staff procurement*. The explanation, although not obvious (since most professors seem to be unaware of it), may be found very easily in the workings of the prestige system.

The relationship between departmental prestige and the personal prestige of department members is reciprocal. Over a period of time, each man's personal prestige in his discipline is a partial function of his department's prestige, and vice versa. It becomes vitally important, then, to maintain the prestige of the department by hiring only individuals who seem likely to enhance it, since a decline in departmental prestige will be experienced by each individual member as a decline in his own prestige. Chapter 8 will discuss this mechanism in more extended perspective.

Chapter 6

Procedures

OF

Recruitment

The process of faculty recruitment cannot be understood or adequately described without attention to the details of hiring procedures, which turn out to be extraordinarily complex and elaborate. Just as the overdevelopment of some feature in the rituals of a preliterate tribe tells us a good deal about the fundamental orientation of that culture, so the analysis of hiring procedures may clarify our general view of the values held in the academic profession.

Open and Closed Hiring

A distinction must be made between the two kinds of recruitment in general use—"open," or competitive, hiring and "closed," or preferential, hiring. In theory, academic recruitment is mostly open. In practice, it is mostly closed.

In the theoretical recruiting situation, the department seeking a replacement attempts to procure the services of an ideal academic man. Regardless of the rank at which he is to be hired, he must be young. He must have shown considerable research productivity, or the promise of being able to produce research. He must be a capable teacher with a pleasing personality which will offend neither students, deans, nor colleagues. In order to secure the very best man available, the department simultaneously announces the opening in many quarters and obtains a long list of candidates named by their sponsors. When a sufficient number of high-caliber candidates have applied for the position, the department members sift and weigh the qualifications of each most carefully in order to identify the one who best meets their requirements. This is the model hiring situation. It is a stereotype of the profession, and it actually occurs in a small percentage of cases. Indeed, some elements of the model situation are present in almost every vacancy-and-replacement, but the outlines are blurred and distorted by a host of other factors.

The most common of these distorting factors is the preferential treatment of some candidates, based on an association between themselves and the hiring department. For want of a better term, it may be called nepotism, although the word is perhaps excessively strong. According to one of the dictionary definitions, it is the "bestowal of patronage by reason of relationship rather than merit."

The seven themes below describe the varieties of nepotism, or closed hiring, which were discovered in the sample. Themes 2 and 4 appear least often, twice each, but Theme 3 is found in more than one-fifth of all hirings.

Nepotistic Themes

1. He had help from his home institution.
2. He knew the man who left.
3. He knew someone here.
4. Someone from there was here.
5. Someone from here was there.
6. He was on the scene [doing research, as a visiting professor, etc.].
7. He'd been here before [as a student, staff member, etc.].

It is not difficult, despite the taboo, for a man with the appropriate disciplinary connections to go soliciting a position. The taboo, it would appear, is quite real (since there are statements that men who solicit positions are rejected from candidacy in some departments), but it can certainly be evaded if things are done discreetly. The technique is to solicit while avoiding the appearance of solicitation.

> "He has a number of friends in the department there— who had been trying to talk him into coming down for a number of years, so I suppose he just indicated his availability."

The crucial factor here is possession of the appropriate acquaintances in the discipline to whom one's availability may be indicated. These are the connections by means of which one is freed of local institutional ties. In our sample, 52 percent of assistant professors and 61 percent of associate and full professors were reported to have done no solicitation for the vacancies. The correlation between rank and solicitation is inverse and approaches statistical significance.

Discrimination on racial or religious grounds is a luxury in the hiring process which seems to be practiced only when there is a surplus of candidates of quality. It is *always* institutional. We know of no instance of a disciplinary discrimination system. As suggested elsewhere, women tend to be discriminated against in the academic profession, not because they have low prestige but because they are outside the prestige system entirely and for this reason are of no use to a department in future recruitment.

With the exception of a few disciplines which enjoy the privilege of hiring in a truly international market (Spanish studies, for example), the importation of scholars from abroad is a sign of a very tight market in a specialty.

The major universities may seek men from abroad before they will seek them from the minor league at home. Failing to discover a candidate to their taste in a foreign land, they may decide not to hire at all; or they may even hire a woman, who, being outside the prestige system, cannot hurt them. Not even as a last resort will they recruit from institutions with prestige levels much below their own.

The Process in Practice

If we turn from the model recruiting situation to examine what usually occurs, it may first be noted that there is considerable evidence that both vacancies and appointments are disturbing to academic departments and often result in a cumulative turnover of personnel. This is to say that the occurrence of a vacancy, especially when coupled with a search for a replacement, increases the probability of future vacancies in the same department. The hypothesis is supported by a statistical study of faculty turnover which we undertook in one of the institutions sampled. The apparent explanation of this circumstance is that the personnel process frequently provides an evaluation of either the departed man or a candidate which is inconsistent with the self-evaluation of some other member of the department, thereby turning his thoughts to greener, or less stony, pastures.

Another event which occurs frequently in the personnel process is the intrusion of outside influence upon the department. For example, a nepotistic appointment may be blocked when an outsider, usually the dean, requests the reopening of the field for further candidates. Factions within a department will often do the same thing, seldom opposing the man whom their rivals have put up for candidacy but muddying his inside track or obstructing it completely by the insistence that other candidates, better qualified, may be found if the search is extended somewhat.

We may also note that many academic men seem to be, as one respondent put it, "passively on the market" all the time. This is to say that they are not soliciting positions actively but will listen to any proposal which comes their way. This is, of course, one way for the individual professor to resist institutional authority, and it is sometimes cited as one of the academic substitutes for unionization.

Another interesting phenomenon is the convention of coyness in the hiring process. Note it in the following quotation.

> "Offers never come directly from the meetings. Academic jobs are done more coyly; you let it be known discreetly that you are available; the actual contact is later."

There is, as a matter of fact, a great deal of coyness in the recruiting process, but mostly on the side of the hiring parties, encouraged by higher administrators. It is very seldom seen in candidates. Ideally, both parties to the negotiation are supposed to be mutually friendly and ingratiating. The candidate usually is, and genuinely so. The university cannot be. It believes it has too much at stake, and the uncertainties of buying a less-than-perfectly-known quantity loom too large. This institutional anxiety can lead to coyness on a grand scale.

> "His name had been brought to the attention of the President there. They met at the home of a friend of his, by accident, seemingly. The President then made him an offer when he went there to make a talk."

Festina Lente

When we examine the specific procedures of hiring in the American university, they turn out to be almost unbelievably elaborate. The average salary of an assistant professor is approximately that of a bakery truck driver, and his occupancy of a job is likely to be less permanent. Yet it may require a large part of the time of twenty highly-skilled men for a full year to hire him. The reader is invited to consider the following report:

> "We had discussed the problem many times in staff meeting. We did a great deal of thinking on this. Our first step was to bring together a committee. They met a number of times trying to decide the qualities to be looked for and then to dig up suitable people to fill the role. After a number of meetings, it was boiled down to five men. One man notified us he couldn't be considered. The other four were brought here at intervals of a week or two. They met with each member of the staff and discussed their specialty. Lastly we invited each to give a paper. We brought in heads of other departments and members of the administration to hear them. They added their impressions to our own. We quickly centered on two men. It was difficult to decide; they had highly contrasting interests, abilities, and accomplishments. There were two or three staff meetings before the vote. The needs of the department were examined. We asked ourselves, 'Do **we** need glamour or promise?' "
>
> "The four men who came each spent about half a week with us. The committee had got out an elegant and complete biography on each man prior to his visit. The vote was taken the week following the appearance of the last man. The Chairman saw the Dean the day afterward, and the Dean said, 'Go to it,' so the letter was sent that day. The level and approximate salary had been settled between the Chairman and the Dean previously, but it wasn't inflexible. The vote included the assistant professors, since it was made at that level."

Hiring procedures of approximately this complexity and duration are not the exception but the rule. Since they have no apparent ritual function in most cases, the best explanation we can offer is that these lengthy procedures reflect anxieties attendant upon the comparison of candidates by estimation of their disciplinary prestige. The appointment of an assistant professor or an instructor for two or three years does not seem to be of enough importance to the university to justify so complex a system on other grounds.

There is always the possibility, especially in the case of a nationwide search, that the participants are simply advertising themselves within their fields. The following case may be an illustration of this.

> "I wrote to every department in the country that offers the Ph.D. I submitted the vacancy to the professional association's placement bureau and wrote all my friends all over the country. Then I went through the directory of the association and looked for recent Ph.D.s with degrees from good institutions who were located in places which they might be induced to leave, and then I wrote to them and also to the schools where they'd come from."

This is a quotation from a chairman. The commentary from another member of the same department is illuminating.

> "The Chairman's office became a central clearing house for candidates. He *established lines of communication with the leading departments in the country.* He also got information from the association's placement bureau" [italics added].

Some Recruiting Agents

The standard patterns of recruitment appear again and again in respondents' reports. Since no discussion of procedures can be complete without a statement of their purposes and results, the roles of the usual agents are noted below.

In many academic specialties within disciplines there are one or two men who are nationally recognized as leaders. These men sometimes become informal deans in their fields. Through their wide acquaintance, they can place almost anyone in the specialty, although they can seldom deny placement to anyone, since they do not control all the vacancies existing. The excerpt below is an excellent illustration of the prestige and placement function of the dean of a specialty.

> "I wrote to a man at one of the Big Ten schools who is the 'dean' of all the teachers of the subject in this country and asked him for suggestions."
>
> [Interviewer]: "Do you know him personally?"
>
> "No, only by reputation. He wrote back suggesting two people and offering to publicize the vacancy in a journal that he runs. Some time later the man we got wrote him inquiring about positions and he put him on to us."

The Slave Market, an inaccurate (although beloved) figure of speech in wide use among professors, refers in general to the academic labor market and is used in particular reference to professional meetings and conventions. It is a misnomer in most disciplines, for it suggests the sale of professor-flesh upon the block with particularly high value being placed upon muscles and endurance. It is specifically applicable only to a few fields, such as English, where there is a great deal of routine and unavoidable undergraduate instruction to be done.

Appearing only infrequently, but dramatically when it does, is an especially elaborate form of procedural elaboration which might be called the Puppet Show. It occurs when a department *really* wants a specific man and is uncertain about being permitted to hire him. In general, it seems to develop in colleges where deans exercise their authority capriciously, for in the cases reported there is no definite evidence that the dean would have opposed the appointment had it been broached directly to him. The department, however, took no chances.

"In a sense, all we had to do was convince the Dean that the University should pay for him. At first he said he didn't want us to hire anyone at a rank higher than assistant professor. By late February, we'd gotten together the papers on a number of possible replacements. We picked four candidates in the three fields [the departed man] represented. I routed the papers to the whole staff and we had a meeting where we ranked them. Then I wrote the Dean a letter with a paragraph about each man. After the Dean had studied it and given us the green light, we made an offer to the first choice. He'd been taken. We tried then to get the second choice to come for an interview. He was at one of the Ivy League and he decided to stay where he was. We phoned the Dean and said we didn't really want either of the others, the third and fourth choices, and didn't believe we had a chance of getting the man we wanted within the limits he'd set on salary.

"In the meantime we'd brought another man in as a Visiting Professor. In June, I talked to him to see if he'd be interested in staying on. He said 'No.' But he spent the summer with us and had a wonderful time. Well, by that time we'd picked out four more men including two we couldn't get at less than associate with $2000 more than the Dean said we could have. We looked them all over and weren't particularly interested. Then one day this visiting man intimated it wouldn't be impossible to interest him in the permanent post. He asked what I thought the Dean might say I wrote the Dean a letter, about the four men, only this time I headed the list with the weakest and worked up to the strongest of the four. Then I added a paragraph to this effect: 'If the administration should wish to do something outstanding for this department, to bring it once more into the ranks of the best in the country, they might be able to bring in our Visitor as a permanent member.' I saw the Dean about two weeks later. He said, 'That was a very clever letter. I wouldn't hire the first two people on your list and after finishing your letter I could come to only one conclusion.' "

The role of the department chairman in the hiring process is an uncertain one. He may be a servant or a tyrant. The examples below are quite typical:

"I've been the editor of the journal for thirty years. I know what's being published and by whom. I write around to my friends for recommendations. I make a personal contact with a man's friends and my own."

"Both of the men gave seminars, which they were invited here to do. Both were here at least 48 hours. The staff reconvened and jammed through a majority vote—not unanimous, but solid."

[Interviewer]: "Was this an open vote?"

"Certainly the discussion was open. I think I may have requested closed ballots. I believe that's what I did. That's what we're doing now on promotions; they want that secret so if there's any complaint they can't say, 'The chairman didn't do it right.' I believe I have their votes in their own handwriting on file, in case there's an error or ever any cause to defend it before the Dean."

This example of closed but not secret balloting illustrates rather neatly the role of the chairman who is a servant of the servants. One other aspect of the chairman's role in the hiring process needs comment. In a good department, to concentrate the hiring in the hands of the chairman is often to allow him to build a feudal empire. Many medical school departments offer excellent examples. They may be, and often are, professionally excellent, but their members, whatever their private feelings toward the chairman, are never likely to forget they owe their positions and their prospects to him. To be the chairman of a bad department and to be solely responsible for hiring, on the other hand, is to be gray of hair and ulcerous of stomach from the constant and frustrating effort to secure suitable candidates or approval for unsuitable ones.

As far as the data of this study permit us to judge, the presence of a university committee in the hiring process is likely to impede the already complex procedures, sometimes to the point of breakdown. The situation is often recognized by the working professor.

> "The Dean has a committee that does these things [evaluation of candidates] all over again. It's a farce, in my opinion. It should work, but it doesn't. They've made some awful appointments. And they've made some mistakes and promoted the wrong people. I think it's lopsided in practice. They've prevented some good appointments and allowed some bad ones. It doesn't work as well as it should. We overruled the Dean's committee last year, had to call the President in Tokyo to do it. I don't like to do this sort of thing, but in this one case it seemed so desperate we went ahead. We were about to lose a whole group of men over the matter of whether to promote one of them or not."

Note the insistence in this quotation, representative of many, that the committee system "should work, but it doesn't." There seems to be no sure way for men who are members of one discipline to check their judgments of a man in another. Knowing neither the prestige nor the bases of judgment of the men recommending the candidate, the members of the committee must resort to their own friends in the discipline or to marginal persons in it (who are more likely to talk freely to outsiders) to arrive at an appraisal themselves. These appraisals will almost certainly be distorted (from the department viewpoint) by the pressure of interdisciplinary rivalries.

The following quotation gives a glimpse of the possibilities of elaboration that lie in this direction.

> "There is a series of steps: I have a personnel committee composed of three full professors, one associate professor, and one assistant professor. When we have a vacancy, the committee makes a search. We have a card file with the area of interest noted for each youngster at every major institution in this country and abroad. We go through that and cut the list to about ten. Then we also have a brief vita on each of them in a larger file—we go through that for the ten and if any of them are really good, we'll go to our central files and get their dossiers. Then we'll call the chairman of his department and ask if he'd be interested. If he is, I go to the Dean and get his permission to nominate him. I make the nomination to the Dean and he sends it to the central budget committee of the academic senate. They appoint an ad hoc committee composed of two men from this department and three from outside. This committee goes through all of our documents on the man and gathers all other possible information on him, and then writes a highly confidential report on him which goes back to the budget committee, which reviews it. If they pass it, it goes back to the Dean and he reviews it. If he passes it, he sends it to the Provost, who reviews it, and if he passes it, he sends it to the President. The President reviews it and if he passes it, it goes to the Board of Regents for decision."

Further comment seems superfluous.

The function of placement bureaus in the recruiting process of major universities can be summarized by saying that prestige is attached to the non-use of their services. This is less true of the university's own placement service than of commercial agencies (which exist somewhere in the darkness of an academic limbo beyond Siberia), but even these are mostly patronized by aspirants with degrees in education, a discipline which, in the view of many academic men, occupies a special Siberia of its own. The contamination of these users has passed to the bureau itself, for reasons which become evident upon analysis.

Recommendations are read primarily in the attempt to ascertain the disciplinary prestige of the candidate. The first consideration for any hiring department is to safeguard itself against a ridiculous choice, the public knowledge of which could lower the departmental reputation at one blow. The unwritten, essential, and elemental rule of hiring, then, is that the candidate must be disciplinarily respectable before he will be considered at all. It is exactly this elemental respectability which no placement service can guarantee, unlike the private letter of recommendation which demonstrates the subject's respectability by the very fact of its existence. As a result, there is a tendency in most fields for only the weakest candidates to use the services of a placement agency. Only where the "slave market" prevails can the placement bureau safely be used by a major department. In such cases, the prestige of the department depends upon the senior men and is relatively unaffected by the juniors.

Hiring Procedures in Perspective

When academic hiring procedures are viewed in perspective, their most striking feature is the time and effort which most departments devote to appointments, including the appointments of junior men, who tend to be transient and unimportant to the department. It has been noted that in most cases the procedure seems to have no ritual significance, although there are some instances of its being used to manipulate a dean. We should also note that if the procedure is too prolonged and agonized, it may pass the point of no return, and the department will find itself unable to make a replacement because any candidate suggested will be vetoed by a remark to the effect: "But is he as good as that young Smith whom we turned down three years ago?"

We have suggested that what the department attempts to do in hiring is to establish the candidate's prestige-potential—his value for future staff procurement. The elaboration of procedures is in part explained by the fact that there are no objective means by which future prestige can be measured. Prestige, it must be remembered, is subjective, consisting, in essence, of what other people think about a man. It may be more important to the department than the qualities of the man, observed in themselves. The academic labor market is an exchange where universities speculate in future prestige values, based on yet undone research. By attempting to hire men whose value will increase at more than the normal rate, they hope to purchase future institutional prestige below the market price. However, since most universities and most departments tend to get the candidates whom their actual prestige deserves, and since they are normally subject to the Aggrandizement Effect, they are very frequently dissatisfied with their purchases.

It is generally believed among professors that democratically administered departments are happier, or more efficient, than departments administered in other ways.

Table 6.1 describes the relationship between department ratings by chairmen and department participation in the hiring process. It is apparent that a more or less oligarchic participation is the mode, regardless of depart-

Table 6.1

Department Rating by Departmental Participation

(N = 131 departments)

Participants in appointment process	DEPARTMENT RATING	
	% High	% Low
Chairman only	10	16
Chairman and some members	52	61
All members	38	23
Total	100	100
Number	69	62

ment quality, but that departments having higher ratings tend to be more democratic in this respect.

The Merits of Candidates

A part of the hiring process often hidden within the overlapping layers of procedures is the actual evaluation of candidates on their merits. The following sensible non-sense is an excellent summary of the way the market for futures is viewed by many of its most active traders.

"We take a good look at their letters and then when they're down here we look at them and talk to them and then we take a good look into our crystal ball and pull out the best man. In other words, we're completely subjective about the whole thing.

"It's usually fairly simple. You can tell from a ten-minute conversation if a man will be a good teacher. The thing that is perturbing is trying to forecast what their scientific career is going to be like on the basis of the same conversation. What counts is drive and imagination. You can have pretty good luck, though, this way. We hired a man this way three years ago who has proved to be the outstanding man in the country of those who were available at that time.

"We can't afford to hire any other way. There is no other way of judging a man's research and scholarly capacities. It's extremely time-consuming, but it works."

Despite the occasional recognition that the process of evaluation is subjective, the overelaboration of procedures which characterizes the whole system of recruiting often represents a dogged attempt to achieve consensus at any price.

"We pass the recommendations and vita and stuff around to the whole staff—everyone on the full-time staff—and they look it over. If there are too many applicants, I may do a little weeding first and throw out the obviously unsuitable ones. Then we write and get opinions from the men we know we can trust with whom they've worked or in their home departments. Then we invite two or three of them down here in a rank order of preference, and everyone gets a chance to see them and talk to them, and we ask them to give a seminar paper for an hour at a staff seminar. Sometimes during the time they're here, a day or two, everyone gets a chance at them and really works them over, in particular with regard to what they have done and are doing in research, what their research attitudes are, that kind of thing. Of course, if they have publications, everyone reads those, or most of us do. And we have a party and pour a couple of drinks into them if they'll take them, and see how they are when they're loosened up a bit. Then we take them in to the Deans of the College of Letters and the Graduate School and let them have a look at them. Then after they go home, we have a staff meeting and really chew them over and everyone gets a chance to have a say and contribute what he thinks of the man. Every man in the department has the blackball privilege, although of course he has to be able to state his reasons. We respect them, too; doesn't matter who they come from if they make sense. We can't afford to have brawls within the department."

The blackball device, mentioned above, may help to insure department harmony, but it probably tends to favor men with neutral characteristics. This is not always an asset, even in a democratic department.

Throughout the information on candidate evaluation, the human element obtrudes in singular ways, sometimes comic, and often pathetic.

"We had one young woman come down here from one of the Big Ten. She had the M.A. and was working on her doctoral dissertation and we would have very much liked to have gotten her, but when she saw the Dean, he turned her down. He didn't like the way she was turned out, thought she was too stylishly dressed. We had thought she looked very lovely."

"We invited one and he came and made a right good impression on everyone. But there were certain complications about him. He was a little older. He had two children. He wanted the job very badly. There was some thought that we ought to have him. Others thought that in this area we couldn't make the job comfortable enough for him. We decided to see at least one of the others before choosing. He had no publications although he did have a good book in manuscript awaiting printing. The second one we looked at had a good publication record, he was younger, and a bachelor; he made a good impression on everybody. After he left we had a department meeting and chose to make the offer to him."

"The Dean and I decided on $4600. He had a wife and three children, so we went higher than ordinarily. The Dean is a humanitarian; he is humane as far as he can be."

One of the most time-honored of all of the evaluative devices in use is that of having all the staff members of the department above the rank at which the replacement is to be made meet to decide upon a man. This keeps the hierarchy hierarchical and reduces the probability of invidious comparison between the emoluments offered the new man and those of present members of the same rank.

Even under the best conditions, the evaluation of candidates is beset with uncertainty. If judgment is made on the basis of a visit, the judges get no view of that research ability which is chiefly sought. If the candidate is judged on the basis of his recommendations, the judge must not only determine what those recommendations really mean but must also evaluate the disciplinary prestige of the recommending scholars.

The Decision-making Procedure

The process of evaluating an academic man is a peculiar one, as has already been indicated. Our respondents' attitudes upon the subject are perhaps best characterized by what they do *not* look for in candidates. Note the following:

> "We don't care about his academic record, we rely on ability."

> "Letters of recommendation, that's all we worry about."

> [Interviewer]: "Do you ever use bureau credentials?"
> "Good heavens, NO! We're interested in promise; we'd be suspicious of anyone who applied to us through a bureau!"

> "We don't get anything at all; we do it entirely on the basis of personal recommendations."

As for the actual credentials used in decision making, it is not an overgeneralization to say that departments do not, as a rule, consider teaching, academic records, or theses. Why theses are not read is a puzzling question, since the thesis is usually the only major work which a young man can show and probably represents the best current effort of which he is capable. But they are not read—in the same way that publications are not generally read in the course of his candidacy for a position. Of course, they may be taken out of the library and piled upon the chairman's desk so that anyone who wishes to do so may look at them. The dialogue below is a fair sample of what happens to them there, if anything happens at all.

Q: Are the men's publications read?
A: Oh, yes!
Q: By whom?
A: By the tenure members, at least.
Q: All of them?
A: Yes.
Q: Did you read them?
A: Yes.
Q: Did you read those of the man you finally hired?
A: Yes.
Q: What was the one which you remember best about?
A: Well . . . I didn't read it, exactly. I looked it over. It was in a good journal. Nothing trashy gets in there.
Q: What do you mean by you "looked it over"?
A: Well, I looked at it, looked at his references, read his abstract.
Q: Is that the way the rest of the committee handles the publications, do you think?
A: I think so, yes, they look them over.

The reason why publications, all protestations to the contrary, are not really *read* has been suggested before:

because men are hired for their repute, and not for what that repute is purportedly based upon. Men are hired, to put it baldly, on the basis of how good they will look to others. It is assumed that the long, grueling training demanded for the Ph.D. guarantees a satisfactory quality of teaching and the quality, if not the quantity, of a man's research. There is very little point in trying to determine how good the man *really* is, or even how good the department opinion of him may be. What is important is what others in the discipline think of him, since that is, in large part, how good he *is*. Prestige, as we have remarked before, is not a direct measure of productivity but a composite of subjective opinion. This is explicitly recognized in many interviews.

> "They don't have to submit credentials. We all know of them. What others think of them is the most important criterion."

> "We are only interested in people whom the members of the department would be quite competent to assess."

It may also be said, in the light of the analysis above, that an academic man's career is pretty well determined by the time he has reached the age of forty. Opinions of him by then will have crystallized and will be so widely diffused that the possibilities of changing them will be slight. Disciplinary prestige is a feature of a social system, not a scientific measurement. It is correlated with professional achievement but not identical with it. A man may, for example, publish what would be, in other circumstances, a brilliant contribution to his field, but if he is too old, or too young, or located in the minor league, it will not be recognized as brilliant and will not bring him the professional advancement which he could claim if he were of the proper age and located at the proper university. Disciplinary prestige, then, has a social and institutional locus. There are men to whom this has happened in every discipline, and many readers will be able to supply specific examples.

A further illustration of the nature of the prestige order is that a man's prestige in his discipline is often measured by the number of citations he receives from other authors—yet the number of citations received is in part a consequence of high prestige. And lest the reader who is a physical scientist believe himself exempt, let it be pointed out that, although the scientist's prestige is presumed to depend upon the quality of his work, the quality is often a function of the equipment to which he has access —which is at least partly dependent on his prestige. High-energy accelerators are not available to unknown instructors.

Table 6.2 describes the kind of credentials required

Table 6.2

Credentials Submitted, by Rank, in Percent

Credentials submitted	Instructor and Assistant Professor	Associate and Full Professor
Recommendations	81	76
Records and publications	83	96
Interview or visit	48	33

of candidates for the position by rank of the replacement. Its dominant theme is the recommendation and the record —meaning publications. Since publications are not generally read—and the data leave no doubt on this point—we may say that the table demonstrates an overwhelming concern with actual and potential disciplinary prestige.

The haunting uncertainties and anxieties of the selection process are reduced in a few specialties in which professional skill—and, hence, prestige—can be determined by audition. Music is such a field. In these areas we find none of the elaborate procedures which prevail elsewhere in the academic profession. Consider the beautiful simplicity of the following.

> "One of the main parts of the job was to select a performer; have a person come to play. All we needed to know was the way he played, his professional experience, and how well he would fit into the quartet."

A final point of interest is that many of the people most concerned with hiring do not seem to know precisely what the hiring procedures at their universities are. In the same department, procedures often vary from one appointment to the next. It is not unusual for the dean to initiate all personnel actions for one department of his college and scarcely to be consulted in another. The formal procedures of appointment are often unfamiliar to people who make appointments.

Perhaps the precise method of selection makes so little difference to the university because all methods are used to measure, very imperfectly, the same variable, and none of them measures it well. There is no evidence from our interviews that the most complicated procedures produce more satisfactory results. Table 6.3 shows the extent to which the departments represented in the sample succeeded in hiring the replacements they desired. Most of them seem to have done fairly well. Taken together with the evidence discussed on page 167, the results shown in the table tend to suggest that departments get the replacements to which their place in the prestige order entitles them.

Table 6.3

Choice of Candidates Obtained in Filling
Junior and Senior Vacancies, in Percent

| | PLACE OF THE APPOINTED CANDIDATE IN THE LIST OF CANDIDATES | | | | |
Rank at which appointment was made	*First*	*Second*	*Third*	*Fourth and Lower*	*Total %*
Instructor and Assistant Professor	78	11	7	4	100
Full and Associate Professor	80	7	9	4	100

Hazards of the Market

Let us remind the reader of a pair of terms introduced earlier--the open market and the closed market. In the open market, information about vacancies and candidates is given the widest possible circulation, and the selection of a candidate is made strictly on the basis of his qualifications. In the closed market, of course, there is preferential treatment of candidates and limited circulation of information about vacancies.

There is a ceremonial way of canvassing for a roster of candidates. It consists of seeking nominations from the big names, both human and institutional, in the discipline. The ceremony is almost always carried out when time allows, but men are hired where they are found and contracts with them are made in such a variety of ways as to defy cataloguing.

We have spoken before of nepotism in the hiring process. Our data on the extent to which closed, or preferential, hiring occurs indicate that for the replacements made in the sample universities 40 percent of instructors and assistant professors and 61 percent of associate and full professors had some contact with the department before their candidacy. There is a statistically significant [1] positive association between the two variables. This is to say that as the rank of the replacement increases, the probability that he has had some contact with the department to which he goes also increases. In a sense, of course, this is to be expected because the greater the rank, the greater the likelihood that the individual will at least have met someone from the hiring department before. However, in most of these cases, the reported contact was much more than casual acquaintance.

We also note in the interviews a steady insistence that prior contact does not make any difference—*i.e.*, does not unduly influence the selection of candidates. This is made explicit in the following quotation:

> "He had had some with me. His father and I had both been on the faculty at another university together, so I had known him when he was small. But this had absolutely no influence ȯn the appointment. His father is dead now and wasn't in this discipline anyway."

For purposes of formal evaluation, prior association between the candidate and the hiring department probably does not make much difference, since it does not affect his prestige; but, as we have already suggested, certain reasons exist why familiar candidates are preferred to unknowns. In departments rated high by their chairmen, 59 percent of the candidates had prior contact before the replacement was hired, whereas in low-rated departments only 38 percent had such contact. There is a statistically signifi-

---

[1] Chi square = 5.29, 5% level of significance.

cant [2] relationship between department rating and the amount of previous contact, indicating that the better departments are more likely to hire men familiar to them. This is to be expected if our analysis of the rating process is correct; better departments seek men with more prestige; men with more prestige are better known and have a wider acquaintance in the discipline.

Prestige is not rank—which is definite and discrete. One has a given rank or one has not; there can be no ambiguity about it. Prestige, being a kind of average of opinions about a man, is, like any average, subject to distortion by extreme values. Hiring departments, therefore, are most sensitive to sharply negative opinions. A mildly critical opinion may be balanced by laudatory reports, but a sharply negative opinion from someone of high prestige is usually sufficient to destroy a candidate's chances. It is our impression, however, that negative opinions referring to personality factors are less likely to be fatal than those referring to professional ability.

The compilers of rosters are haunted by uncertainty about finding and evaluating men. We suggested earlier that disciplinary respectability is so urgent a requirement in a candidate that some canvassing techniques are not used for the sole reason that they cannot assure this. The result of the uncertainty, of course, is often nepotism, since departments are apt to prefer anyone who is at all familiar to someone who is totally unknown.

There is another uncertainty to be taken account of: the fear of the "Bogie-man Replacement." There appear to be two kinds of bogie-men whom departments fear. The first is the temperamental prima donna, who can wreck a department by his mere presence. He is especially danger-

[2] Chi square $= 5.02$, 5% level of significance.

ous in the tenure ranks since prima donnas—as visualized —will do anything to get what they want. The second, and more conspicuous, bogie-man is the "man who won't fit in." Among the most common qualities sought in candidates are "the right personality," "someone whom we can live with," and the like. The frequent reliance upon the blackball, or the senatorial courtesy principle, is illustrated by one or two of the interviews that we have quoted previously. This concern with getting replacements with whom the department can live, and the rule that a candidate must be *persona grata* to everyone in the department, reflect the fear of the man who won't fit in. On the part of the candidate, "fitting in" involves the acceptance of the values of the department as a peer group and a willingness to defend it under attack from without, especially from higher administrators, whom the department often regards as enemies.

This conception of the department as an embattled band is especially strong in expanding disciplines, in which the process of professional growth makes recurrent demands upon the administration for further funds for new positions, promotions, and research support. The department must, in this situation, be a conflict group, constantly striving to acquire a larger share of the finite institutional budget at the expense of competitors. Such departments are especially wary of "traitors" who will betray departmental secrets to the administration or to its disciplinary enemies. Equally dangerous is the nonconformist, who cannot be assimilated into the defensive structure of the department and who threatens its prestige by operating as a detachable Achilles' Heel.

These threats are given the weight and worry which they receive from professors because each man's prestige is linked to that of his department, and anything which threatens the prestige of the department is experienced as a threat to the individual's ego. There is seldom any feeling expressed that the replacement must be a pal, a "good buddy," to the members of the department, or personally charming; but he must be a reliable member of the peer group. If he is this, he may also be almost anything else he chooses.

So the poker game of personnel is haunted by uncertainty and anxiety. We have several instances where this anxiety about the process has so mounted within departments that even nontenured appointments are put on a short-term basis in order to assure that there will be no problem of disposal, should the replacement turn out to be a bogie-man. Thus we find the title of "acting assistant professor" in increasing vogue at certain major universities. The reader is asked to consider, if he will, the level of anxiety which makes a two-year contract seem too long, so that junior staff must be hired on an "acting" basis in order to shorten their tenure to one academic year at a time. We even have one case of an acting instructorship.

Signing and Sealing

An examination of the techniques of offering also reveals situational stresses at work. In general, candidates do not delay acceptance of offers very long. Universities, on the other hand, are apt to withhold final word until the last possible moment, presumably in case a better candidate appears or something unseemly is learned about the one in hand. It is much easier for a candidate to make up his mind than it is for the institution. (He knows more about the institution than it knows about him.) Table 6.4 describes 158 first responses to offers, according to the mode of the candidate's acceptance. It shows that most of the

Table 6.4

Acceptance of Job Offers by Candidates

Mode of acceptance	Percent of Candidates
Oral tentative	5
Written tentative	6
Oral definite	22
Written definite	67
Total	100

candidates did not hesitate to commit themselves. The details of the interview responses confirm this finding. In general, the candidate tends to abandon his hesitations at an earlier point in the sequence of events, whereas the department is often undecided up to the moment an offer is made, and even beyond. *The immediate outcome of the academic personnel process, in the typical case, is a happy candidate and a worried department.*

Despite their general reluctance to reach a final decision, universities tend to make initial offers rather early in the process in order to get candidates to commit themselves. The offers are often extremely discreet in their wording and detail. A very common proceeding, for example, is to ask the candidate to accept the position before the university has offered it:

> "I sent the nomination to the Dean, briefed him on what we wanted. The Dean recommended him to the Vice-President, the Vice-President to the President, and the President approved the nomination, so I called him to tell him so. I had, prior to that time, secured a letter from him saying that he would accept the position under the conditions stated if it were offered. That's S.O.P.—we always do that."

The candidate in this case, is ethically bound to accept the position and not to seek others while waiting. The university is not bound to make an offer, and the failure to do so can always be attributed to higher officials whom the candidate does not know. All questions of ethics aside, this procedure is a vestige of the buyer's market of an earlier era, and it can impose real handicaps on departments forced to operate in the seller's market of today.

Table 6.5 describes the amount of bidding or haggling

Table 6.5
Negotiation on Terms of Job Offer,
by Rank, in Percent

Negotiation Reported	Instructors and Assistant Professors	Associate and Full Professors
No	84	71
Yes	16	29
Total	100	100

about terms and conditions after reception of an initial offer. It again demonstrates that candidates are not the coy parties in the hiring process and have little inclination to bargain.

Chapter 7

Patterns
OF
Choice

We have thus far discussed the recruitment process as if it involved only the candidates, the department, and a few university officials. In fact, there are all kinds of other influences which impinge upon the transaction. Some of these have to do with the internal system of the university—for example, its rules and folkways for budgeting. Others reflect the external system of the disciplines, most notably supply and demand in particular specialties.

We can distinguish two general types of replacement processes in large-scale organizations: the "serial" and the "discrete" replacement. Serial replacement—upgrading to fill vacancies from below—is the typical bureaucratic replacement process as found in industry or the military establishment. For a variety of reasons, it is seldom found in universities, but it does occur occasionally, as illustrated by the quotation below.

> "Well, what we actually did was to promote an instructor to fill the assistant professorship he left and then at the same time added another man as an instructor."

The Rules of Budgeting

One explanation why serial replacement does not occur more often has to do with budget psychology and procedure. In most cases, to promote an instructor to a vacated assistant professorship is to lose some money from the total departmental budget, because it is unlikely that the newly appointed man will be given a salary as high as his predecessor's. The department, of course, has not lost anything of immediate value, since the position is still filled at the same rank as it was previously, but any drop in the budget total is viewed as a decline in the department's relative position vis-à-vis other departments in the university. A new man appointed from outside, on the other hand, is likely to receive somewhat more than was paid to his predecessor, on the general theory that some premium must be paid to attract a migrant from another university. This increase represents a net addition to the department budget. (Compare the figures in Table 7.1 with the previous salary figures for vacancies which are given in Table 5.2.)

In the accepted philosophy of academic budgeting, every position is created for a specific man, who is hired to fill specific departmental needs—*i.e.*, every replacement is a "discrete" replacement. The budgeted position, however, becomes the "property" of the department, complete with an appropriate rank and salary range. An English department, for example, may see the instructor who specialized in Milton rise to a full professorship over a period of years, on merit and seniority. When he dies, resigns, or retires, the normal expectation will be that another full professor must be hired to fill the vacant budget position.

As a result of this prevailing expectation, it is relatively easy for a department to keep its old positions when

Table 7.1

Mean Salaries of Replacements*

Rank of replacement	*Salary at four universities lowest for this rank*	*Salary at four universities highest for this rank*
Instructor	$4248	$ 4727
Assistant Professor	5255	6098
Associate Professor	6409	8199
Full Professor	9050	12,167

The table was constructed in the following way: Reported salaries at which replacements were made were averaged for each rank at each institution. Median institutions were then removed and the remaining eight institutional average salaries by rank were divided into high and low groups and averaged for each group into four higher-paid and four lower-paid groups. Reported salary ranges and medians by rank were:

	Instructor	*Assistant Professor*	*Associate Professor*	*Full Professor*
Median	$4575	$5500	$7150	$11,000
Range	$4000-5000	$4700-7500	$6000-8800	$7400-12,500

they fall vacant, but the creation of new, additional, budget items is always difficult. It is a curious fact that the same administrators who enjoy almost complete discretion in the establishment of new faculty positions abstain from exercising much control over the replacement of vacancies—the nerve center of budget control. The fact that most American universities seem to expand without any plan or pattern has been remarked upon many times. The principal reason is that few of them have any procedures for removing surplus positions from their budgets. The occurrence of a vacancy provides an opportunity for budget review which is seldom used. Careful administrative control over the replacement of vacancies, such as is exercised in one of the universities sampled,[1] is likely to lead to the reorganization of the entire institution.

Table 7.2 supports this contention. It shows that, according to our respondents, 38 percent of the vacancies

Table 7.2

Rank of Vacancy by Need for

Replacement, in Percent

Direct Replacement Needed	Assistant Professor	Associate Professor	Full Professor	Total Sample
No	36	31	54	38
Yes	64	69	46	62

which occurred did not call for the appointment of a successor to do the same work. Table 7.3 is a tabulation of the rank of the position filled by the need for replacement of

Table 7.3

Rank of Replacement by Need for

Replacement, in Percent

Direct Replacement Needed	Instructors and Assistant Professors	Associate and Full Professors	Total Sample
No	38	23	33
Yes	62	77	67

[1] In that university every replacement is treated essentially as a new position and must be specifically justified before it can be made. The argument that there had been a similar position before is not accepted as evidence that there should be again; positions, thus, are totally discrete and attach only to individuals; no department has a table of organization with positions in it.

the former incumbent and is remarkably consistent with Table 7.2. According to respondents' reports, 33 percent of the replacements actually made were unnecessary in terms of continuing the functions of a predecessor. This is not to imply that these replacements were all made wastefully, however, since in many instances the men hired were chosen for their competence in other areas of interest to the departments—for example, in teaching fields which had not previously been covered. The department, in other words, may seize upon a vacancy as a chance to reorganize, although not to reduce, its activities.

Table 7.3 suggests one relationship not apparent in Table 7.2—namely, that senior staff are less likely than junior staff to be replaced unnecessarily, perhaps because their appointments are subject to more thorough administrative review, or perhaps because the possibility of carving two junior positions out of one senior vacancy is likely to suggest itself when replacement is unnecessary.

These tactics are inherent in the budget policies of most universities. When a department develops a need for additional services, extensive documentation is usually prepared, on the department's initiative, to justify the proposed new position. If an existing service becomes obsolete, however, departmental initiative in returning the surplus to the university is unheard of and would be regarded with general suspicion. There is a tendency on the part of all those who participate in budgetmaking to regard new positions, or funds for them, as scarce and expensive, whereas old positions are thought of as "budget items," which in some sense have already been paid for by incorporation into the total of the university's charges. This attitude is reinforced by the budget procedures in general use. When it is proposed to add a new position to a department, the request may be scrutinized minutely at every administrative level right up through the Board of Trustees; at the same institution the department chairman may not even need permission from the dean to fill a vacancy. But if a department ever gives up a budgeted position, it can not expect to get it back in the face of the argument that: "You've been getting along without it."

In our entire sample of vacancies and replacements, there is not one instance of a department's refusing to make an appointment because it was unneeded, although it was admitted to the interviewers that 38 percent of the vacancies did not call for direct replacement. This finding calls to mind an episode at one of the universities in our sample when, several years ago, requests for suggestions for the establishment of new positions and the abolition of old positions were circulated to departments on parallel forms. Several million dollars' worth of new positions were proposed, whereas the total recommendations for abolition covered only one clerical position with an annual salary of $2100, located in a department other than the one which suggested its abolition.

There is a real problem here. Everything once built into a university budget continues to claim support with great tenacity. In a bureaucracy, people are promoted into already existing jobs, and the aging of individuals does not automatically change the table of organization. In universities, however, jobs get promoted along with the men holding them. The academic budget, in its usual form, is an historical accident and, unlike other budget structures, its existing distribution of positions rests on no rationale at all. Thus, in the case of the English department cited previously, it is an accident that the man who formerly taught Milton stayed long enough and behaved well enough to become a full professor, and the department may have no reason at all to continue the position at that level. But at that level it is almost certain to stay until another historical accident alters the pattern.

The flexible and unpredictable table of organization poses a recurrent problem for the administrator—one that is aggravated by a seller's market: shall premiums in rank and salary be offered to attract new men? If so, what is to be done about the resentment of men already on the staff? This dilemma is faced squarely by the respondent in the quotation below.

> "I have a man in mind who is almost a duplicate of the man who left, but he is younger. I can't bring him in as an associate; it would cause friction among my assistants. But I can't get him as an assistant. I don't know what I'll do."

Few departments practice the most effective technique for getting the men they want: that of selecting them in advance of the need for their services. We can now see why they do not. Appointments are usually tied by administrative procedure to vacancies, and if there are no vacancies, it is often intolerably difficult to obtain permission to make new appointments. If a department wishes to hire a specific individual, the probability is very low that he will be dissatisfied where he is at the same time that it has a position to offer him. If a department were able, over a period of years, to hold out a standing offer, the probability of eventual consent would rise very sharply.

The Specification of Duties

Another factor in the replacement process is the specificity of the duties attaching to the vacant positions: to what extent are they determined in advance of the appointment? In practice, the range is wide. There are vacancies for which the duties are specified in minute detail. In other cases, a position is left completely open, without even the rank's being decided in advance of the selection of a candidate. In the present sample duties were specified in advance for 77 percent of junior and 86 percent of senior staff replacements. It would appear that some specification of duties is made in most cases, with more detail for senior appointments. Perhaps it is more important to specify the duties for senior professors in advance, because so much less control may be exerted over them once they are hired. For all ranks, there is probably much of the kind of control suggested in the following quotation:

> "We look for a man with interests that we think will lead him where we want him to go, and then we tell him, 'Go where you want to.' "

A second reason for attaching more specificity to senior positions is that this makes it easier to justify them to higher authority, for, although the need for a replacement is seldom questioned, there is always the possibility that it may be.

The Decline of Teaching

In general it appears that the more objective the content of the discipline, the less identification there will be of men with courses. It is relatively rare in physics, for example, for anyone to "own" a course, but this is common in English and the humanities.

The quotation below illustrates the usual mechanism for reducing course loads in a department. Its special interest lies in the fact that the average teaching load has been falling precipitously in all the major universities in recent years. One way in which this is accomplished is to bring in a man with a course load lighter than average for the department "for the first year." We have found no cases in which loads were raised after that year. This is an academic variant of the general industrial principle that it is always possible to raise wages and fringe benefits for employees but very difficult to lower them again. The effect of teaching load bonuses offered to new appointees is ultimately to lower the normal teaching load for all the members of the department.

> "We knew what we wanted, the job we wanted to fill. The Chairman would make a considerable effort to lighten his teaching load for the first year."

There is also considerable evidence to support the belief that, along with the general reduction of average teaching load in the universities studied, teaching itself is regarded more and more casually. The following series of quotations illustrates the new attitude, perhaps another result of the increasing orientation toward the discipline.

> "It was just ten more hours to go back into the pool of teacher hours. I wouldn't be able to trace it back. Somebody shifted to cover the advance courses, and the introductory courses were taken over by part-time instructors."

> "We would regard his classes as so many undergraduate courses to be taught, but we could replace his teaching with a graduate assistant or an instructor, as far as that goes."

> "These positions tend to fluctuate. You have a position which stays open several years until you find somebody who seems to fit it, hire him, and then let him do as he pleases anyhow. The emphasis in this department, as in most departments in this discipline, is on research. There's always somebody to handle the teaching; one looks for a good man in terms of his research and productivity. One lets a position lie

open and shifts viewpoints readily. They don't have a tag on
the position."

Motives for Migration

In general we may say that an institution's attractiveness to a candidate is determined by what it can offer him
in the way of prestige, security, or authority. The specific
attraction is a function of the candidate's own situation, so
that, for example, prestige is usually the stronger lure for
men on the way up, whereas security and authority become
more attractive to men on the way down. These are the
major "attractiveness" themes, each of which is illustrated
by one of the quotations below.

(Prestige)
"Harvard—he'd only been away from it for a period of
months when the first word came they wanted him back, and
the pull was terrific."

(Security)
"Well, I think he thought he wanted to teach in a smaller
institution, a place where the major effort would have to be
teaching, with very little emphasis on progress in research.
My guess is that the most important thing was the chance for
permanence."

(Authority)
"I think the free hand to organize and administer things
was as he wanted. When you are head man you have the
chance to put some of your own ideas into practice. That was
probably number one, the challenge it offered."

The overwhelming majority of men who leave posts
in major universities do not go to universities of similar
standing. They move either up or down, institutionally
speaking. When they go up, it is generally to an increase
of both personal and institutional prestige. When they go

down, they are often compensated by an increase in security or authority.

We have thus far concerned ourselves almost exclusively with major universities. Since many of the departures made by men in the sample had minor institutions as their destination, this form of retreat needs to be considered more closely. We can see several motives. In the first place, a given amount of disciplinary prestige will go a longer way in a small institution than it will in a large one. A man's prestige losses may be cut, therefore, in this way, if he has been unable to meet the norms of the major league. A record of three or four papers published may represent failure in a major university, but it is reckoned as a fair amount of scholarly activity in a minor state university and makes a great reputation in a local college. The principle of status conservation, of course, also tends to bar any subsequent return to the major league.

Unlike executives in the industrial world, academic men almost never go down in rank when they descend institutionally, for in order to preserve the formal interchangeability required for the solidarity of the discipline, a full professor at any university must be regarded—for some purposes—as the equal of a full professor anywhere else. An associate professor from one of the lesser members of the Big Ten who receives an associate professorship at Harvard is regarded as having been promoted, whereas an associate professor from Harvard who comes to the same university is almost certain to be given a full professorship. However, the former individual would probably never have been offered the Harvard position if he had been a full professor at his midwestern university, since he could not decently be offered less than a full professorship. Needless to say, any associate professor from a leading university who goes to a minor institution will receive a full professorship there. Migration in the other direction is less common, since a full professorship in the minor league is not worth a similar appointment in a great department, and nothing less than equivalent rank may be offered. The minor league is, for the most part, identified with teaching and the older academic values but also, and perhaps unfortunately, with intellectual provincialism. The "bush league," that host of small denominational institutions, teachers' colleges, junior colleges, and the like, lies quite outside the academic world of the major universities. Downward exchanges are rare, and upward exchanges are unheard of.

The retreat into the minor league, however, is eminently respectable. We find that major league administrators—together with a small number of eminent scholars —sometimes follow this path in search of security in their declining years.

> "He'd been Dean of the Graduate School, came back to teaching, and found himself shunted to one side. He had lost track of what was going on in the department. People assumed he was not abreast of developments and did not consult him. He felt that his prestige and influence were shrinking as a consequence. He may have taken that deanship [at a smaller institution] because he felt he didn't have full influence anyhow."

A recurrent theme used to explain the retreat from the major league is that of the "big duck in a small pond." This phrase (the out-size animal is sometimes a frog) appears very commonly in the interviews apropos of downward movement on the institutional prestige scale. It seems to stand for the opportunity to cut prestige losses which was mentioned earlier.

Downward-bound men often leave academic employment entirely without sacrificing their training and skills.

There are a certain number of nonacademic employments available in almost every field. These help to maintain a kind of equilibrium, since the demands from outside the discipline drain off surplus and unsuitable personnel. The range of activities to which academically trained men put their talents is almost impossible to summarize. They go into industry and industrial research in large numbers, operate their own businesses, join consulting and research agencies, and perform many kinds of unusual and esoteric services for the public at large. Physical anthropologists, for example, are employed by the armed services to assist in the design of uniforms and equipment. More home economists are employed by food, drug and appliance companies than by academic institutions. Chemists and physicists are always in short supply in aircraft factories. English professors are snapped up by government agencies to write technical manuals.

Although these positions on the fringe of the discipline may pay much more than what their incumbents could ever earn in an academic post, the acceptance of such employment is always interpreted by a man's colleagues as moving down in or out of the profession. One of the peculiar facts of this situation is that men who take this path are often spoken of by their remaining colleagues in the past tense as if they were literally dead—as, indeed, they are from the disciplinary viewpoint. They are rarely able to return to the academic employment, and when they do, any minimally respectable academic position is regarded as an opportunity for them.

For the men of the major league, the road out of the academic profession is generally a one-way street. It is taken only by those on their way down, except for a few men at the very top of their specialties who have no further place to go within the bounds of the profession. The ex-

planation for the unidirectional character of this movement seems to be that a man's prestige is made up mostly
of opinions about where he is, where he has been, and
where he is going. When he leaves his institutional locus,
the bases of judgment are lost. The status he may attain in
a nonacademic job is not convertible to disciplinary prestige because the nonacademic unit for which he works lies
outside the system of the discipline.

In some cases, the road out of the profession is taken
by men who may be said to have missed the train for Siberia. The period of transition is often a traumatic one, as
suggested by the case below.

> "He's here in town. I don't think he's doing anything. For
> a while he sold calculating machines."

Men moving within the major league usually go either
upward or downward to departments of definitely higher
or lower prestige. When men move up, they may have to
pay for it with the loss of privileges, and even some financial sacrifice. Consider the following:

> "His old position was immeasurably superior. He was pro-
> fessor and chairman in a small college. His salary and stand-
> ing were much higher; it was a deliberate sacrifice on his
> part."

The respondent here has apparently not considered the
fact that the replacement's former position could not have
been "immeasurably superior" or he would not have "sacrificed" to get out of it. The values of institutional prestige
make the sacrifice worthwhile. Just as men pay to get out
of the minor and into the major league, so they are rewarded for leaving the majors for the minors. It is almost
axiomatic that willingness to move down is rewarded by a
promotion of at least one rank and a salary increase. In
terms of local status and the family budget, it is often pos-

sible to live better in "Siberia" than at the great institutions.

The prestige system is often implicitly recognized in respondents' comments, and the recognition is occasionally explicit, as in the following quotation, in which the speaker considers and then rejects one by one some other possible explanations for the movement of a colleague.

> "He was at a southern university. We gave him $1000 more, but he would have made some of that up there, had he stayed. His perquisites here are quite in excess . . . but that's a subjective statement. He was getting along very well (professionally) there. We could get him because we are who we are. He has a climate which greatly favors research here."
>
> [Interviewer]: "What about rank?"
>
> "I think he was an assistant professor there; to me that's a minor matter."

In many places in the interviews, we find evidence of the reluctance of departments to hire men from slightly stronger departments. Most hiring seems to be done from departments which are either much stronger or slightly weaker. Hiring from a slightly stronger department involves the risk of being sent the rejects or of having to pay prices higher than the men are worth in order to compensate them for their loss of prestige in coming one or two rungs down the ladder. When hiring is done from much stronger departments, it is the rejected aspirants of the stronger departments who become available; their prices are also high, but the prestige of the department from which they come may be sufficient to compensate. The advantage of securing men from departments slightly weaker than the hiring department are obvious in this analysis: the slight prestige margin of the stronger department often enables it to hire the best men of the other on favorable terms. We have also noted the consequences of the Aggrandizement

Effect, by which a department will see itself as equal to others which in the consensus of the discipline are slightly better. The traces of this effect can be found throughout the interviews, a usual complaint being that "although they're no better than we are, we've never been able to get a man from them." The department which attempts to fill a vacancy for some time without success is probably trying to hire better men than its prestige deserves.

The following quotation illustrates two of the problems of the recommendation system: that a recommendation is no better than its author and that weaker departments tend to get the rejected candidates of stronger ones.

> "We took him on the basis of the enthusiastic support of an outstanding professor at Harvard. That's very important. If Princeton pushes a man, I know it means I'll have to look somewhere else. I don't trust Columbia either, or Chicago. With one or two exceptions in each department, those bastards are shysters; they'll say anything about anyone to get a man placed. There's one man at Harvard and one at Yale that I know I can trust. I won't take a man from either place without their say-so."

This chairman's plaint—in a department not among the very best in its field—is obviously the result of long experience with candidates sent him from the great universities.

When respondents were asked why they believed replacements were willing to come to their departments, their answers fell, in general, into three thematic categories:

1. This was the best he could get.
2. This was as good as anything else he could get and had incidental advantages for him.
3. He just felt that it was time for him to be moving—that he had been there too long.

In most cases of the "time to be moving" theme, the disciplinary prestige of the subject had grown to the point where his former department could no longer reward him adequately. Table 7.4 describes the attractiveness of the posi-

Table 7.4
Rank of Vacancy by Attractiveness
of Position Elsewhere, in Percent

Attractiveness of new position	Assistant Professors	Associate and Full Professors
Unattractive	13	4
Attractive	67	59
Extremely Attractive	20	37

tion to which men went by their rank, as reported by respondents in the departments which they left. The significance of the table lies in the fact that in 91 percent of the vacancies, the positions to which men went are seen as attractive by their former colleagues and in the positive relationship between reported attractiveness and rank of vacancy.

Similarly, in many, many cases, respondents in the new department see the reasons for a replacement's move in the attractiveness of their own department to outsiders. We suspect that this is what the replacements have told them and that the men of the department simply accept the compliment. The quotation below is an interesting illustration of this. The respondent first considers and then discards the possibility of dissatisfaction with the old position, and finally attributes the move to the attractiveness of the new department.

"Well, he *was* in the College of Education there. Then, aside from that—although that's reason enough, God knows!

—this is a pretty good department and it was a fine opportunity for him."

Supplementary Opportunities

Another significant matter which cannot be overlooked
in the comparison of any two academic positions is the
opportunity which the incumbents may have to do outside
work in addition to their institutional duties. Since this
kind of activity can markedly improve a professor's level
of living, it ought to figure largely among the motives for
mobility. What part does it play in the marketplace?

In some cases, outside consulting is restricted to the
senior members of the department.

"Opportunities are good for the older people—better leave
that undefined—and, say, fair for the younger ones."

On the other hand, some departments seem to encourage
outside commitments whenever possible.

"He's young—I've thrown him some speaking engagements
and we're trying to get him some research money for this
summer so he can get himself established."

"We took it upon ourselves to help him get into organized
research projects and let him have leeway. It was a moral
obligation. An interdisciplinary research group was contacted
to see if they could throw something his way, and another
research group gave him their list of foundations to use in
looking for opportunities."

But some departments systematically discourage consultation or outside research commitments.

"Such opportunities would not have been discussed. No inducements. We want a full-time full professor to devote his
full time to us, including his research. If he gets research
grants, that's all right, we could probably adjust."

There is probably a functional reason for the restriction of consultantships to senior staff. Since salary is a significant academic prestige symbol, it would not be appropriate for the junior members of a department to have incomes exceeding those of the senior members, as might occur if consultantships were available on an equal basis. Although access to outside work can be one of the significant privileges of the professor, it is also a lever for the exercise of authority over senior staff. In many institutions, permission to accept a consultantship must be obtained from or through the dean.

These matters are usually discussed rather surreptitiously, if at all, in job negotiations, although they are occasionally of tremendous importance to the participants. Because of their extra-professional nature, they apparently cannot be overtly identified as perquisites in job negotiations. Consultantships range in type from long-term, high-income arrangements (governor of the Federal Reserve Bank, in one case) to occasional and insignificant opportunities like this, reported by an anthropologist:

> "An advertising company wanted some consultation on totem poles for a cereal box."

Table 7.5 enumerates the opportunities for consulting

Table 7.5a
Rank of Replacement by Opportunities
for Consulting, in Percent

Opportunities for consulting	Instructors and Assistant Professors	Full and Associate Professors
No	37	24
Yes	63	76
Total	100	100

available to the replacements of the sample, but questions about the volume, nature, and stipends of consulting cannot be answered from our data, despite a mass of related material.   ●

Table 7.5b
Opportunities for Consulting,
by Subject Area, in Percent

Opportunities for Consultation reported	Sciences	Social Sciences	Humanities
No	12	18	63
Yes	88	82	37

Chapter 8

Selecting
THE
Replacement

"The biggest thing is that other people think well of him. It's like choosing a wife; you want one that other people will admire too. It's hard to tell exactly how good they are; the opinions of others are presumably related to promise as a scholar. We're also influenced by apparent brightness and possibilities of stimulation for us—and they're supposed to be able to teach, I guess.

This perspicacious quotation summarizes most of what needs to be said about the ranking of candidates for positions, but some qualifying comments may be made. First, the older attitudes, which placed great value on teaching and teaching ability, are not entirely dead, even in the major universities. Especially in departments of the humanities, the teaching requirement still has considerable meaning, even under the pressure of the universal demand for research.

"We want a good academic record, good personality, promising teacher. That's the first requirement, although if he can show while he is here that he also has promise in research, his future with us will be much more secure. But

he's got to be a good teacher with an interest in teaching in this department."

The reader may be bothered, as we are, by the nagging question: Where men are hired to teach only on the basis of their research productivity, what happens to teaching? With the exception of some humanities departments and a few atypical natural science and social science departments, the answer to this query takes two general forms: (1) Teaching doesn't matter—it isn't important; and (2) There's nothing to worry about—any Ph.D. can teach.

"Our requirements are purely mathematical. No one gives a damn if you can teach."

"He must have done well in his theory courses, and we try for, and are interested first and foremost in, his potential for research. We assume that if he got through school, he'll have the ability to teach, unless we hear specifically to the contrary."

So much, with the exceptions noted, for the criterion of teaching competence.

Who Is the Fairest?

To know the qualifications desired in candidates is not necessarily to know the qualifications by which they are chosen. We have seen that disciplinary prestige is the measure of evaluation when the roster of candidates is being assembled, but other qualities may be sought when the roster is in hand. In general, higher administrators are responsive to "names," hoping thereby to add to the prestige of the university as a whole. Departments tend to prefer younger men with promise in order to gain the reflected glory of their development and to avoid the reorganization which usually takes place·when an eminent stranger is imported.

> "The Dean wants big names. I'm interested in promise. We have a tendency to have too many chiefs and not enough Indians."

This situation also reflects the fact that the university, as an organization, is less sensitive than the department to prestige nuances. Bright young men have much less visibility to deans than to chairmen.

There are usually only two major qualities identified in candidates: prestige and compatibility. We have analyzed the case for prestige at some length. Let us allow a respondent to make the case for compatibility:

> "He had to have a good background in the subject, Ph.D., some experience, research-oriented, bright, hard-working. Good social person, nice person, happily married. Those last two are important; you let some shit in, or someone with marital problems, Christ knows what'll happen. We have trouble enough with the things that happen normally without a paranoid around or someone's wife trying to lay everybody. We hire men to keep; we think personality is tremendously important."

The issue of teaching vs. research pervades the academic marketplace, and compatibility is linked in the minds of professors with teaching, in part because compatibility with his students is one of the prime qualities of the teacher, and in part because compatibility—like teaching—is an aspect of the local system and is foreign to the discipline. This linkage between teaching and compatibility probably explains the fact that in departments strongly oriented to research the inquiry about a man's compatibility is often put in negative terms: "We wouldn't want someone who. . . ," down a list of specific offenses. Note the summary handling of personality factors in the following quotation from a natural science department.

> "There were no other considerations except the possibility of his achievements in research. If his personality were known to be bad, there might be an objection raised, but it would usually be couched as an objection to him as bad scientifically. The mere fact that he is a nice person is never taken into consideration. A tendency to assimilate power is the only personality trait that I have heard discussed."

In departments which emphasize teaching, on the other hand, certain kinds of compatibility are positively required.

> "He had to be an assistant or associate professor. Sparkling personality, keen intellect, integrity; a man able to both teach and write, trained in French history but with breadth permitting him to teach other things, ability to lecture to large classes, but able to guide individual research."

To a large extent, the specific qualifications departments desire in their replacements are different from their criteria of acceptability. Men *have to be* within a specific prestige range to be acceptable to a department, but when that has been determined, other criteria come into play. An interesting illustration of this is found in the quotation below, from one of the strongest departments of its kind in the country. Here the prestige of the department is so high that high prestige is taken for granted in its candidates and the only qualifications mentioned are those of compatibility.

> "A reasonably pleasant personality, an ability to make people like him right off—that's part of a good teacher's job. We look at that part of his personality rather carefully. 'Presentableness,' I'd look for that."

At the other end of the scale, somewhat similar comments are often heard. As departments get fuzzier in their measurement of productivity and prestige, extraneous qualifications increase in importance. Here is an excerpt from a department regarded as substandard in its university and its discipline.

> "We wanted a man who would be competent, a personality which would be effective in classroom teaching, ambition and scholarly promise, socially presentable, and a wife who was also socially presentable."
> [Interviewer]: "This is important?"
> "Yes, very important. These people have to take a place in the community, after all."

Another point of interest is that compatibility seems to be of less importance in urban institutions than in universities located in smaller communities, even in the major league.

> "Many of them live out in the suburbs and come in in car pools. Communal life is lacking; only five live within shooting distance of the campus. The Chairman invites students to his home; there aren't many who can do that."

Finally, in the major universities the Ph.D. is seldom mentioned as a requirement; it is taken for granted. In weak departments, it may be a stated requirement.

> "Oh, a Ph.D. That's the union card. Some publications and the proper personality."
> [Interviewer]: "Was all this put in writing?"
> "No, everybody knows that this is the basis. They are presumably people of intelligence and wouldn't send a man without the Ph.D. and probably not one without some publication."

When all is said and done, the compatibility requirement in the major universities is essentially defensive. It becomes far more important as we descend the institutional scale. The more rudimentary or parochial the program, the less emphasis on professional competence and the greater the demand for saints. Consider the following prescription from a rather weak department.

> "Solid experience in practice, interest and ability in teaching, flexible, outgoing, and friendly. At least an M.A. A person secure enough that he wouldn't become defensive, able to take secondary roles, able to take leadership in community planning, with an avid interest in his specialization."

As a rule the qualifications communicated to candidates are not the ones on which they will actually be judged. In formal statements of job requirements, a great deal of lip service is given to teaching. It is possible, of course, that one reason why teaching ability does not weigh very heavily thereafter is that information about it is difficult to obtain. In any case, the qualifications defined in advance tend to be broad and nonspecific:

> "Personality, plus achievement, which leads to the fact that we ought to have an outstanding man in our small field, one who could impose himself on the field, most commonly by publication."

A curious fact which emerges from those sections of the interview dealing with the job qualifications of candidates is that there is virtually no mention of experience. Nonacademic experience is usually deemed either irrelevant or undesirable, and even serious research experience —unless leading to signed publication in the professional journals—is seldom taken into account. Teaching experience, of course, is difficult to summarize and even more difficult to evaluate. The lack of interest in experience is especially notable when one realizes that in almost every other occupation working experience is what makes up a career. In the academic profession, the record consists principally of publication, secondarily of former affiliations. Any experience which is convertible into disciplinary prestige is rapidly converted. Any which is not convertible is thought to be irrelevant. Prestige is something one *has,* whereas experience lies somewhere in the past. The ideal academic career is marked by rapid promotion, and as few other events as possible.

In some of the statements about qualifications, there is, rather surprisingly, some evidence of anti-intellectual bias. Brilliance, especially in young men, is suspect unless it is turned into the universally acceptable coin of productivity. Although unexpected, this attitude is understandable. Members of the academic profession are, after all, preselected for intelligence. The unintelligent are not usually attracted, and when they are, are seldom able to meet the requirements. A high I.Q., then, has no special value in an academic discipline, being a necessary condition for entrance. Anyone who attempts to establish a claim to prestige based on his intelligence but not supported by the accepted evidence of his usefulness becomes a threat to his colleagues. By suggesting that prestige without production is possible, he introduces alien criteria. He usually leaves the profession or is packed off firmly ("He was brilliant but . . ."), if regretfully, to Siberia.

Given the gap between the stated qualifications and the working standards of professional evaluation, how do departments choose among a number of suitable candidates when the field has been narrowed down? The selection is not without problems, especially when a department has ascertained the prestige of two or more candidates to be approximately equal. Since they can no longer be selected on the basis of disciplinary prestige, the tendency is for many other qualities to enter into the decision. Every kind of criterion imaginable is mentioned in interviews; the quotations below give some idea of their range.

"That's difficult to say. You've got the factor here of three or four men equally trained, so it comes to the subjective factor that he grates on you because he's got dirty nails."

"He was chosen in part because he was particularly eager to come."

"There were certain complications about him. . . . He wanted the job very badly."

"He started in the Eighteenth century and was working backward. There were some others in the same period, but their direction of thought was forward, not back, and they'll run into the modern period where everyone has plenty of people."

"We discarded both of the other active candidates on the basis of their approach to research. One seemed to go through all of the motions, but . . . it was kind of a subtle thing, all of us noticed it . . . he talked a good research but didn't seem to understand why the motions were the right ones. The other was a statistician who seemed to be so happy to be able to apply math to his data that he didn't get beyond its manipulation. He didn't seem to ask any questions at all about what it *meant*. Just engrossed in the elegance of his methods, I guess you'd say."

"He played the recorder. That was the reason we hired him."
[Interviewer]: "Because he played a recorder?"
"Yes, we thought that would be nice."

The point, of course, is that two equally prestigeful and amiable candidates pose a neat problem for the department whose selection devices are all directed to the measurement of disciplinary prestige and compatibility. When these are not at issue, anything at all may provide a basis for choosing between Dr. Tweedledum and Dr. Tweedledee.

Supply and Demand

Table 8.1 shows the number of candidates mentioned

Table 8.1

Department Rating by Number of Candidates Considered

	DEPARTMENT RATING		
Number of names considered	*% High*	*% Low*	*% Total Sample*
1	25	18	22
2 - 5	20	16	18
6 - 10	23	13	18
Over 10	32	53	42

for possible consideration in the total sample of vacancies and replacements. It is of interest to compare the range of search with the prestige rating of the department. The findings shown in the table are mildly surprising but not inexplicable. In general, strong departments consider fewer candidates than weak departments. As shown earlier, they have more prior contact with their candidates. Presumably, their greater bargaining power enables them to get the men they want, and their greater prestige makes it more likely that candidates will accept an offer. Weaker departments consider more men. They must, in effect, cast a wider net in order to secure any fish. Many of the candidates they attract will be unsatisfactory or will ultimately refuse an offer. There is, too, in the case of the weaker department, the possibility that the desire for self-advertisement leads to searches more widespread than necessary.

However, as we see from the table, the opposite situations are by no means rare. The strong department which wishes to consider a number of candidates may use its extensive contacts in the discipline to canvass the nation in a search for the "best man of his age" in a specialty. The weak department with only one or two candidates is probably unable to elicit any other applications, or experience may have taught it that any man available to it should be employed as quickly as possible before he gets away.

No discussion of the academic market can ignore the classic variables, supply and demand, even though their influence is sharply limited by institutional factors.

One of the expectations with which the investigation began was that only the strong departments would be likely to get their first choice of candidates available. As we saw from Table 6.3 however, an impressive 79 percent of the departments sampled got their first choice candidates, whereas another 9 percent were able to hire the man of their second choice. This suggests that some sort of equalization of availability of candidates takes place, and our theoretical assumptions prompt us to look to the prestige model for an explanation. We know that the major universities have the most graduate students and may, in a sense, be said to control their supply.[1] But the number of spon-

---

[1] The number of institutions granting nonmedical doctorates has doubled during the last few years, amounting now to nearly 200 institutions, including a good number known as colleges, such as Bryn Mawr and Arizona State. However, fourteen of these have long produced more than one-half of the total. These are California, Chicago, Columbia, Cornell, Harvard, Illinois, Iowa, Michigan, Minnesota,

sored people—who are those most likely to secure positions
in major universities—must be in rather direct proportion
to the number of sponsors; there is, therefore, a tendency
for new Ph.D.'s to enter the market in a cohort, with a distribution of prestige roughly proportional to that of their
sponsors. Those new men from the most prestigeful departments with the most prestigeful sponsors will be distributed to the vacancies in departments of high prestige; the
group on the next lower prestige level will probably seek
and find positions in departments with slightly lower prestige, and so forth. Thus, departments at every prestige
level tend to be supplied with recruits whose potential
prestige matches that of their own members.

Let us recall for a moment some relevant features of
the classical market model. The employer determines what
wages he can offer (on a profit and loss calculation which
need not concern us here) and has labor available to him
in proportion to the relative attractiveness of his terms.
Skilled workmen are able to command more attractive
wages (or conditions of employment) than less skilled workmen. Workmen have a range of wages which they are willing to accept, and employers have a range of wages which
they are willing to pay. The market price for labor will be
found in the area of overlap of these two ranges. If wages
fall, some workmen will quit the market and new employers will be able to enter, thus decreasing the supply of
labor available and increasing the demand until wages
cease to fall and a new equilibrium is found. If wages are

New York, Ohio State, Wisconsin, and Yale. They accounted for 56
percent of the total doctorates granted during the years 1930 to
1946, and 53 percent of those granted from 1948 to 1955. Among
them they have awarded more than 50,000 doctorates in the past
generation. W. H. Cowley, *An Appraisal of American Higher Education,* Stanford University, 1956, mimeographed, unpublished.

raised, more workmen will enter the market and some employers will leave it, thus increasing the relative supply of labor and decreasing the demand until wages cease to rise.

The academic marketplace, as we have seen, departs from these conditions in several respects. For example, outside employers are able to absorb a large body of academically trained workers, attracting them by higher salaries, but these workers are unable to return, regardless of the fluctuations of wage rates, because of the prestige system of the major universities. In several areas touched by this investigation, minor colleges surrounding a major university are paying considerably higher wages than the dominant institution without attracting personnel from it in any significant numbers.

In the academic marketplace, employers are not, as in the model, viewed as interchangeable. There are few institutions at the prestige level appropriate for each worker. Further, the worker does not choose his employer; the employer must seek him out. The worker must take what is offered at the appropriate prestige level, since he is unlikely to receive offers from institutions at higher levels and unwilling to accept offers from lower levels. The prestige system protects him from demotion and from loss of pay but not from the cost of living, with the familiar result that professors are hard-pressed in times of prosperity and relatively affluent during depressions. Academic men are probably less interchangeable than the personnel of other professions. (What English department can have any use for a microbiologist?) When prestige requirements are added to specialty requirements, the supply of men for any given job is found to be very limited. It can not be readily expanded in response to market fluctuation because of the ten years needed to train a scholar.

The Impact of Replacements

One of the questions which the respondent was asked in the course of the interview was whether, in his opinion, the specific replacement made would have any long-range effect on the department. This question was most often answered "yes,"—in 59 percent of cases in high-rated departments and 60 percent in low-rated departments—but without much useful detail. The vagueness of these responses about the effect of appointments on the department's long-range program is perhaps explained by the fact that departments seldom have long-range programs. The program is almost entirely a function of the roster of the department. It cannot be closely predicted because there is no way of forecasting all the changes which may occur through death, unexpected resignation, or future appointments.

Although the responses to the question of impact are interesting as expressions of attitude, they may not always be very meaningful. Departments are collections of people assembled to perform numbers of relatively unrelated duties. Some of the anxiety attaching to the selection of men for membership probably results from the fact that every appointment changes the department as a work group. Since the group is relatively small, every appointment will have some impact. To choose a man for the department, then, is to modify one's own future as a member. Every addition or subtraction implies some change in the distribution of teaching duties, of privileges, of research activity, and of sociometric preferences. Strictly speaking, the department has no collective task, but its members and their activities are closely linked, and they think of the department program as if it were a single task.

The changes which may be made by the addition of a member are often foreseen as attracting more graduate students to the department. Whether this actually happens or not, we do not know, but the belief that it does happen is important. The data previously presented with regard to discipleship (see p. 71) tend to support the belief that individual teachers attract students to a department. But the notion often expressed that no man affects the continuity of the department is equally plausible—especially in departments of high and long-established prestige, where the addition or deletion of even an extremely eminent man may have no discernible effect upon the reputation of the department. In leading departments, there is a long time lag—it may be ten years or more—between changes in the personnel roster and the resulting changes in prestige. In weaker departments, one appointment or resignation can make a real difference. In the quotation below, the respondent is pointing with pride to the increase in his department's prestige which the acquisition of a man from the major league will effect. The recruit's impermanence in his former position does not seem to diminish the triumph.

> "He's one of the best in his area in the United States. Hiring him lifted this department into the big league. It's the first time we ever stole anyone from the Big Ten. He was on a temporary appointment in a research capacity. There was no intention on their part of making it permanent."

Personnel Poker

As we have suggested, institutional prestige does not affect the ease or difficulty of faculty recruitment in the major universities very much. Departments are able to get most of the men they go after and—with some reservations —these men are acceptable to them, for the tendency to self-aggrandizement is not of sufficient magnitude to nullify the process by which departments and men are matched. When departments are compared according to their success in hiring the candidates they select, 86 percent of departments rated "among the first five in the country" were able to obtain men of their first choice, but 82 percent of all other departments were also able to do so.

This question leads us to examine the "poker game" phase of the recruiting process—negotiation about wages and working conditions.

It is obviously to the candidate's advantage to raise the institution's initial offer, and the stronger his position in relation to the institution, the more likely he is to do so. An unusually successful case of a candidate's raising the offer is recorded below.

> "I had initially offered $6000-6500 as associate professor. He didn't feel that that was quite adequate. He also wondered if he couldn't be made full professor. I went back to the Dean on salary, and he agreed to $7400 as associate professor. I wrote the man that in my opinion that was the best we could do, and he took it."

Generally, however, universities resist raising by the candidate and claim that they do not permit it. Of 108 responses to a question as to whether any bidding or negotiation occurred during the hiring process, only 25 indicate any attempt at modification of the terms by the candidate.

There are really two varieties of poker played for faculty services. One involves the matching of offers from other institutions for men already on the staff and was discussed at some length earlier. The rules of the game are explicitly recognized by administrators, and the language conforms to our poker analogy:

> "No bidding, no terms and conditions. As a matter of fact, it has been the Dean's general policy not to get into degrading bid-raising deals; I think it's a good one. In a case where

you're losing a man, you make up your mind what you're willing to pay to keep him and make a considerable jump in the salary offer. Usually the other institution can't offer more than a token raise over that, which wouldn't even cover what it would cost him to move."

Offers from nonacademic employers, like offers from Siberia, will usually not be met. Since such organizations operate outside the academic prestige system, they will not be dealt into the game, and a professor who brings so disreputable an offer to the university in an attempt to improve his position may well be told to take it.

"He also had an offer from some government lab. We made a flat offer to him and that was it. We don't get into a position to raise the thing; no deals to raise a hundred and get him. Even if you get an offer from outside, they don't hustle to give you a raise. That's a protective device; I think it's a good one. It has caused headaches and hard feelings sometimes. There have been cases of people who work this thing, where the offers haven't been bona fide offers. We consider a man's value when the budget is made up; it's hard to change afterwards."

Another variety of poker is played when candidates for academic positions attempt to improve upon the salaries offered them. These attempts are usually not successful, for the same reasons that meeting the bid of a competing institution can normally stop the play; the hiring university, in order to make sure of the candidate, usually "goes the limit" which it is willing to pay in its initial offer. If he asks for more salary or better terms thereafter, he is likely to be refused. Additionally, attempts by the candidate to raise the terms are regarded with suspicion by the university and are apt to prompt serious questions about his desirability. (Departments see *themselves* as attractive to candidates, it must be remembered.) The quotation below probably represents the usual response to a candidate's attempt to raise.

> "I never bid. I refuse to. That's a tradition I inherited from the previous chairman. He made the offer and no other offer. We're never willing to change terms. It's done in some places, much less here. We fit the man into the scale, make the offer, and that's the end. We've lost people that way, but they know there's no possibility of haggling."

This approach to the game is taken by most departments. They may, occasionally, increase an initial offer by a few hundred dollars if the candidate's own department has done so, simply to show that they regard him as highly as the department from which they are trying to take him.

The "no haggling" policy, however, refers only to salary and rank. Working conditions and equipment *can* be bargained for, and they frequently are.

> "Well, we offered him a certain salary. But he was concerned with the research equipment here and said that he couldn't come unless the money were available to replace some of the equipment. So $20,000 was made available to him to refurbish the lab. That was done by haggling."

Academic poker is a three-handed game. Within the limitations described in an earlier chapter, the department from which a man is being taken may regard the loss as a threat to its prestige and bid actively, if there is no objection to him personally and some likelihood that it may succeed. The department that seeks to hire him away, on the other hand, sees its own attractiveness as the fundamental reason for the candidate's interest and often will refuse to raise its initial bid when financially able to do so. One device sometimes used to avoid the bid-raising round is illustrated as follows:

"Before you check with the administration on the actual appointment of a specific individual, you can be honest and say to the man, 'Would you be interested in coming at this amount?' and he says, 'No, but I would be interested at *this* amount.' "

The candidate who opens the round has often tipped his hand by letting his own department realize that he is actively in the market. If they feel rejected, they may drop him, and he will find himself forced to accept the outside offer, whether he wants it or not. As we have noted, his own department may be willing to bid to keep him—once, but not repeatedly.

In sum, the candidate is unlikely to be able to raise the terms very much. On the other hand, it is commonplace for the department to lower the terms initially demanded or expected by the candidate. Among other reasons for the greater flexibility of the candidate is that he speaks for himself, whereas the department cannot, as a rule, speak for the university. This restriction does not apply to the few issues on which two-sided bargaining often takes place, such as hours and courses to be taught, or laboratory equipment.

We have no cases reported in which a candidate was successful in an attempt to raise the proffered rank. He is of course, often able to raise his rank in his home institution by playing poker with another, since the receipt of the outside offer has already changed his prestige at home. It was noted earlier that unsuccessful candidates for positions may acquire some of the prestige of the position aspired to through the fact of their unsuccessful candidacy. The same effect also operates sometimes in the case of a man who rejects offers from other institutions. The fact of his desirability to others—who will, of course, have offered some advantages over his present position in order to en courage a move—raises the candidate's prestige in his home department to the point at which improvement in his position is clearly called for.

Table 8.2 compares the form in which the offer was

Table 8.2

Rank of Replacement by Form of Offer, in Percent

	RANK AT WHICH APPOINTMENT WAS MADE		
Form of offer	*Instructors and Assistant Professors*	*Associate and Full Professors*	*Total Sample*
Oral inquiry	15	12	14
Written inquiry	17	9	15
Oral commitment	22	14	20
Written commitment	46	65	51
Total	100	100	100

made with the rank of the position involved. Its significance lies in the fact that in 29 percent of the total number of cases the offer was in the form of an oral or written "inquiry" as to whether the candidate would be interested in certain terms. We have remarked that institutions like to play their cards close to the chest, and this type of offer contains an element of sharp practice. Academic poker is often an exciting game, with a wide variety of stratagems.

"We are at a slight disadvantage in having to make our offers far enough ahead so that we can get the acceptance and then go through the rigmarole of nomination because that gives other institutions time to outbid us. The dean is now encouraging everyone to follow the policy of making offers over the telephone instead of by letter so that one can get a line on what the man is thinking and whether he's got any other institution after him."

"In order to get the people you want, it is sometimes necessary to reduce their teaching loads. There is a state law requiring a certain number of hours' load but there are ways
of getting around it and the dean is perfectly willing that we
do it. He informed me that it wasn't necessary to insist on that
load when making terms with men."

Seniority and Merit

Table 8.3 summarizes the answers received to the

Table 8.3
Rank of Replacement by Predictability of
Next Appointment, in Percent

New appointment predictable *	Instructor and Assistant Professor	Associate and Full Professor	Total Sample
No	15	23	17
Yes	85	77	83

* Includes "partly predictable."

question, "Can you foresee the circumstances of the next
major appointment which will be made in your department?" The fact that in 83 percent of the responses to this
question there was some discussion of future appointments,
usually related to future vacancies, appears to support the
hypothesis that the "push" is stronger than the "pull" in
academic migration. Many of the responses to this query
describe men moving toward a point of no return in alienation from their colleagues, who can say something about
the process but seem quite helpless to do anything about it.

"Yes, within six years there'll be a major appointment to
be made. The question will be: shall we have two men to
represent the area or shall we let it drop back to one? I

wouldn't venture to say what the outcome will be. This area's represented by a man who is hard to get along with. I can foresee it; I hope I die before it comes up. It's hard to defend the rights of the younger fellows who will carry on when the older ones are gone."

In many cases in which departments are unable to fill vacant positions in a reasonable time, the reason for the failure is that they have been seeking men too prestigeful for themselves or their universities.

"I suspect there probably won't be any more appointments for a long time. They've been trying for some time to get someone high-powered. They won't come. I imagine they'll continue to look for a young man. I don't know why the big men don't want to come; they just don't, for some reason. We have a professorship here, for example, with a salary as good as any, around $14,000. People won't touch it."

The respondent in this case is probably quite correct in thinking that the salary attaching to the position in question is "as good as any." The problem may be that it is not good enough to compensate a man with the prestige the department demands for the prestige-loss he would sustain in coming to the department, which is not first-rate. Further evidence for this point is afforded by the fact that the larger number of the unfilled vacancies in the sample call for full professors. Few assistant professorships remain empty long.

In all organizations, real difficulties occur in the reconciliation of seniority and merit. These problems are especially difficult in the academic profession, in which the assessment of merit is not subject to control by the local organization. The standard organizational dilemma, then, is magnified by the fact that seniority is acquired in the institution, whereas merit is fixed by the discipline. In most organizations, a senior who has not acquired sufficient merit to warrant promotion at the time his seniority demands that he be promoted is given token merit to rationalize the necessary promotion. It has been alleged that the military services, for example, have formal protocols for exactly this purpose, and it does appear to be true that a large number of senior officers sport the ribbon of the Legion of Merit on blouses otherwise unadorned. It is highly probable that an academic department faced with a similar predicament will not be able to find a satisfactory solution.

> "Last year I brought in a man at a salary higher than that of the three others who were already here. I had to; it was the only way I could get him and he was worth it. The Dean promised to raise their salaries this year, to get them above his. We may end up losing someone as a result. There's been some feeling about it, and if the Dean doesn't keep his word, I don't know what will happen."

Indeed, one of the motives for salary secrecy is the concealment of situations in which seniority and merit are out of alignment.

There are four active seniority scales in the academic profession, based respectively on age, on length of service in a specific rank, on what may be called "professional age" (reckoned from the date of the Ph.D. or from the date of first publication), and on length of service in an institution. Sometimes all of these may be applied in different situations in the same university, depending upon the conditions and the subject.

They can lead to complications. Who has precedence for promotion—the oldest associate professor, the man who has been with the university longest, the one who has been an associate professor longest, or the one who received his degree first? [2] To this inequitable tangle, add the complications of a differential prestige structure within the discipline, and another within the university itself, and anguish for someone is certain to follow.

In the major universities, merit is determined for the most part by disciplinary prestige. An operational definition of merit might be a man's worth to other institutions plus elements of local and private evaluation. The reconciliation of conflicting claims of seniority and merit is always one of the fundamental problems of academic policy. Such problems often occur in very acute form when someone has been brought into a department at a salary higher than incumbents of equal merit, or when there are two aspirants for promotion in a specialty which has room for only one.

As a matter of fact, some conflict between seniority and merit occurs whenever a new man is brought into a department at any level except the lowest—because his appointment changes the distribution of seniority among the other members of the department without changing the distribution of merit among them. A similar problem occurs whenever a man receives an offer from another institution—because this changes the distribution of merit within the department without changing the distribution of seniority.

[2] Compare the relative simplicity of a military seniority system. Military seniority is determined by rank. Between two officers with the same rank, the officer with the earlier date of commission is senior. Between two officers with the same rank and date of commission, the one with the more service is senior, and between two officers with the same rank, date of commission, and time of service, the older is senior. The rules are carried even further, to the point where it is literally impossible for any two persons to have exactly the same seniority—the whole purpose of the procedure.

An academic department is an organized group, and its personnel can be formally arranged by rank and by salary within rank, starting from the top. This array is not changed when a new member enters the department below the incumbent who is lowest in rank and salary. It *is* changed whenever anyone is brought in above this level or when one salary is raised above another or when someone is promoted.

Let us repeat here the principle of the conservation of status, enunciated earlier. *Gains of status are usually, but not always, sought by the incumbents of organizational positions. Losses of status are always resisted.* Thus, when a new member is appointed above someone else in the department, or when one salary is raised above another, the members of the department lower on the ladder than the recipient have lost either present status or a prospect of future improvement. There are likely to be some stirrings among the most junior members of a department when a full professor is appointed, because his coming leaves one less place at the top to which they can aspire.

Chapter 9

Academic Government
AND THE
Personnel Process

It should not be forgotten that these data cover only part of a larger story. All of our information was obtained from members of the departments in which vacancies and replacements occurred. We are therefore compelled to observe the actions and attitudes of the principal actors from the point of view of their departmental colleagues. Needless to say, this point of view embraces only a fraction of what is relevant. A similar limitation must be noted as we turn now to the participation of the higher levels of academic management in the personnel process. These participants are many—deans and assistant deans, administrative committees, provosts, vice presidents, presidents or chancellors, regents or trustees. We know from the general interviews with these officers of instruction that some of them feel directly responsible for hiring and firing and ascribe to themselves a much more active role in the appraisal of faculty candidates than the departments are willing to recognize. The report which follows should be read with these qualifications in mind. It embodies a *departmental* view of academic government.

Who Participates in Faculty Recruiting?

Table 9.1 divides the academic recruiting process into a number of stages and shows the proportion of active participation at each stage by officials in the several levels of the academic hierarchy.

Table 9.1

Active Participants in the
Recruitment of a Faculty Member,
by Separate Stages, in Percent*

Participants	Search for candidates	Evaluation of credentials	Selection of candidates	Consulted before offer	Making offer	Closing contract
Higher Administration	5	3	8	15	27	8
Deans and Committees	76	60	48	85	67	34
Chairman and Senior Colleagues	91	87	83	48	75	75
Whole Department	17	29	40	25	5	—

* A cell value of 100 would equal involvement of the given participants in the given stage of recruitment in 100% of the replacements studied.

Participation of trustees in noncontroversial appointments is usually a formality consisting of the ritualized introduction to a letter: "The Trustees of the University take pleasure in confirming your appointment as. . . ." The few cases in which they were noted as having been consulted before the offer was made occurred in universities which require the approval of the trustees before a candidate may be offered a position. Approval was always routinely given. There were no instances reported in which the governing board of any university refused to approve a candidacy or turned down a recommendation for appointment.

As reported by departments, the president and the vice president also play a formalized and passive role in the recruiting process. In a small percentage of cases, they are noted as making the actual offers to candidates, but this too is usually a matter of form. As the table shows, they occasionally intervene in the search and selection process. The role of a chancellor or a provost is much the same as that of a president in these respects.

The dean is relatively inactive in the search for, evaluation of, and selection of candidates, but he is consulted prior to the offer more than any other individual or group. He may also be quite active in making the offer and closing the contract. His usual responsibility begins with setting the terms which the department will be allowed to offer. He is frequently called upon to approve or disapprove of the department's choice. From the department's point of view, this is the dean's major function, and his office is frequently seen as a place where candidates get vetoed out of candidacy. The restriction of his activity (in the view of departments) to this passive one of disapproving or approving is partly an illusion resulting from the disciplinary perspective of the departments. This is made explicit in the following quotation.

> "We consulted other men in the area and the man who was leaving himself. The Dean was called when we wanted to invite a man up at our expense, and we sent him a dossier at the same time. The Dean's office is primarily a vetoing office, since *he is not a biologist* [italics added]. He only passes on what we initiate."

Deans are very seldom, if ever, asked to initiate candidacies. There are no instances reported where this occurred, although the deans' participation in the recruitment process is quite variable. Whether or not he interferes at any stage may depend upon the department members, since his power over them is in large part a function of the power they ascribe to him. This is to say that a department chairman who assumes that the dean has authority over the selection of candidates may be apt to hand him a slate and ask him to select the one he likes best, whereas another chairman may walk into the dean's office and say, "This is the man we are hiring." Each of them is likely to have his expectations for the dean's behavior fulfilled. Samples of these patterns of chairmen and deans are offered by the quotations below.

> "I took his credentials to the Dean. He looked at them and said all right, whereupon I wrote to the man that I was asking for his appointment. He accepted; then a formal letter was sent. It was approved by the Dean."

> "I wandered in one day and said, 'George, do you want to stay with us and be an Assistant Professor?' He said, 'Sure!' and that was it."

To some extent, the amount of autonomy granted a department in the selection of its candidates depends upon the personality and the wishes of the individual dean. In theory, of course, this is determined by the rules, but in many universities the rules are so obscure or diaphanous that power situations are left to resolve themselves according to the aggressiveness of the participants. The series of quotations below are all taken from interviews in the same college and indicate considerable disagreement about how much authority the dean has and when and how he exercises it.

> "There was no screening committee; it was all between the Dean and I."

"I had to carry the department's choice to the Dean. The Dean has never been known to turn down a departmental selection."

"On an appointment like this, an instructor or assistant professor, we just put it on the budget."

"We got the approval of the Dean and various members of the cooperating department. There was cooperation on the part of some of the other departments too."

"We consulted the Provost."

It is evident that department chairmen are key figures in the recruiting process and seem to have a very high level of activity in all stages except consultation before the offer (which is to be expected, since it is usually they who are consulting others at this stage). The chairman is usually the personnel officer of the department, and there are chairmen who do little else, spending most of their time and energy in recruiting.

The chairman and the senior staff of the department, together, constitute the most active level of the hierarchy. The department as a whole is more active in the opening stages of the process and is most often concerned with the actual selection of the candidates. In the later stages, participation drops off rapidly. This again reflects the conventional model of the situation. Candidates are located and screened by the chairman and the senior professors and are then offered to the department as a whole for selection. There appears to be an effort by most chairmen to obtain consensus on the appointment before the candidate is officially hired. This is sometimes neglected by chairmen who are merely hiring manpower in departments in which the senior staff do not consider instructors and assistant professors to be department members, but as a general rule, some attempt at obtaining a consensus is made.

Official committees do not play a part in the recruiting process everywhere, and their relative influence in the sample is not great. When active, however, they are active throughout the process. As a rule, a campus personnel committee can act on its own initiative in obtaining credentials and letters of recommendation and appraisal, or even in soliciting a list of candidates—activities from which deans normally abstain. The committee, especially when appointed by the dean, also has the covert function of dispersing responsibility for the approval of candidates and, since committee reports are secret in the institutions using this procedure, the committee can become a weapon for the dean to use against the departments. Consider, for example, the enjoinders contained in the memorandum below, from one of the universities studied. Note especially the implications of the italicized sentence in the first paragraph.

MEMORANDUM TO FACULTY APPOINTMENT AND PROMOTION
    COMMITTEES

Your attention is invited to the President's Memorandum, "Instructions of Appointment and Promotion Committees," in which the confidential nature of such committees is emphasized. I am sure you will agree the effectiveness of these procedures, which have been developed out of the experience of many years, depends in part upon the confidential character of the deliberations and reports of the faculty committees. In a recent memorandum, the President explains that "These instructions were worked out with the budget committees and administrative officers, and it was clearly the 'intent' to exclude all others from access to the reports of review committees, because disclosure to the recommending officers of the findings and membership of review committees, which usually include at least one man from a candidate's department, and often several from the same college, *might adversely affect the relationships between committee members and their administrative superiors at the departmental and college level*" [italics added].

To insure that the deliberations of appointment and promotion committees may be given strictly confidential treatment, the following suggestions are offered:

1. The chairman of an appointment or promotion committee should convey personally to the other members of the committee, either orally or in writing, the name of the individual under consideration;

2. Members of appointment or promotion committees should treat the composition of the committee and the name of the person whose appointment or promotion is being considered in the strictest confidence;

3. Supporting material submitted to the chairman of the faculty committee by the appropriate administrative officer should be circulated, when necessary, between members of the committee by means of sealed envelopes or packages labelled "Strictly Confidential";

4. In the event that the chairman of the department of which the person under review is a member is consulted, the chairman of the committee should remind the chairman of the department of the entirely confidential nature of the consultation;

5. Great care should be taken to insure that all documents relating to the discussions and subsequent conclusions of the committee be forwarded to the appointing officer with the recommendations of the committee, and that all preliminary drafts or copies of these documents be destroyed;

6. The actual deliberation of the Appointment and Promotion Committee should, of course, be considered as confidential by all members.

The off-campus consultant is most active in the initial stage of the hiring process, when candidates are being discovered. This, of course, is to be expected, since most departments would resist the influence of an outsider on the final decision. The outside consultant sometimes appears again in the later stages of the process, just before an offer is made. This is normally the result of the activity of an official committee which checks the recommendations of the department by obtaining the opinions of eminent outsiders from the same discipline.

Table 9.2 compares the participation of the various

Table 9.2
Active Participants in the
Recruitment of a Faculty Member,
by Department Rating, in Percent

(N = 157 departments)

	DEPARTMENT RATING	
Participants	*% High*	*% Low*
Higher Administration	36	33
Deans and Committees	96	97
Chairman and Senior Colleagues	92	98
Whole Department	57	39

parties to the recruiting process in departments of different quality. The relationships it shows are surprising. It had been expected that departments of higher rated quality would suffer less outside interference in their selection and evaluation. As the table shows, however, there are no significant differences in this respect between departments rated "among the first five in the country" by their chairmen and all other departments, except that the high-ranking departments report somewhat more participation by the whole department. It is not always clear from the interview reports exactly what chairmen mean when they say that they did consult the whole department. Procedures for consultation vary widely, from the full parliamentary order with secret balloting to the exchange of a few words between the department head and a crony in the corridor.

Some Perspectives on Participation

Table 9.3 compares the participation of the parties to the recruiting process as reported by the chairmen and by the peers. In general, the reports are similar but there are

Table 9.3
Active Participation in the Recruitment of a
Faculty Member, as Reported by
Chairmen and by Peers, in Percent

Participants	Chairmen	Peers
Higher Administration	40	21
Deans and Committees	98	93
Chairman and Senior Colleagues	95	82
Whole Department	47	48

one or two perspective effects which are worthy of notice. The principal difference in perspective concerns the participation of the higher administration, which is reported about twice as frequently by chairmen as by peers.

There is other evidence to suggest that chairmen are involved in a certain amount of consultation with higher levels in the hierarchy about which they do not inform subordinates and which the subordinates do not perceive. This may be the result of a desire on the part of chairmen to appear more autonomous than they really are. The same effect appears at higher levels as well, for two deans of colleges told interviewers that *they,* and not the departments, were the hiring agents in their institutions. In general all three levels—peers, chairmen, and deans—tend to agree quite closely with regard to their own participation and that of levels subordinate to them, but there appears to be somewhat less awareness, on all three levels, of the involvement of levels above their own. Unfortunately we do not have the same kind of specific reports from the deans and presidents that we have from chairmen and peers. Comparison of perspectives on additional levels might be illuminating. It is, of course, to the advantage of the chairman or the dean to conceal his dependence upon the strata above him from those below him in the hierarchy, since the more authority an individual is believed by his subordinates to have, the more likely they are to allow him to exercise it. On the other hand, it is also to the advantage of the chairman to consult his staff on all matters of importance, since they are admirably placed to sabotage his administration.

Promotions, in contrast to new appointments, often occur over the objection of some member or members of the department. If they did not, every rank would be totally subordinate to the rank above, and a system of this rigor cannot be functional even in a military hierarchy,[1] much less an academic one. For this reason there are occasional

[1] In the army, promotions may be initiated by any superior or automatically by longevity. When an individual is being considered for promotion, he is appraised by his immediate superordinate, the commanding officer of his unit, and the commanding officer of the larger parent unit, who is the final authority and may promote against the recommendations of subordinate commanders.

reports of promotions made over the objections of a majority of a department and sometimes without the knowledge of department members.

Few appointments are made in this way, however, because few men will accept an appointment under such conditions. The reason, besides the obviously strained social situation which would result, is that disciplinary prestige is a matter of other people's opinions, and within a discipline members of departments are constantly being asked by outsiders to give their opinions about other members. Much of the conversation at any professional meeting consists of questions and answers about everyone's colleagues and gossip about their work, abilities, and plans. This is the way in which disciplinary prestige is established and maintained; and for anyone to enter a department against the wishes of its members is to prejudice himself in his discipline, for the inquiries never cease.

Stresses Within Departments

It is a favorite maxim of professors that "a professor is a man who thinks otherwise." There is a factual basis for this claim. Scholars are disputatious, almost by definition. The doctorate is still awarded for "defending" a thesis, presumably against the attack of examiners who think otherwise. Many of the quarrels which disturb the peace of the ivory tower are nothing more than fights between two men of incompatible opinions.

Nevertheless, conflict, too, tends to be organized. There are factions in all faculties, and at least some of the factions are the same everywhere. In each of the ten universities, it is a simple matter to trace the lines of schism between:

Young Turks	and	Elder Statesmen
Teachers	and	Research Men
Generalists	and	Specialists
Conservatives	and	Liberals
Pro-administration	and	Anti-administration
Humanists	and	Scientists
Inbred	and	Outbred

Most of these fundamental divisions are likely to be represented in any good-sized department. The relationship between schisms in departments and departmental participation in the major issues which split a university faculty from time to time is too complex to describe here. Academic feuding deserves investigation in its own right.

What concerns us at this point is that there is always an ample supply of standing issues around which personal conflict can crystallize. And crystallize it does. We have no way of estimating the statistical incidence of academic feuds, but we do know that a question to the effect, "What are the important feuds in your department?" seldom draws a blank. Feuds involving senior members are likely to spread to most of the other members of the department before they are settled, or dissipated or the partisans of one faction are driven out of the department. The departmental feud may develop from a clash between two strong personalities or two different viewpoints, or may arise from quarrels over funds or materials or such perogatives as offices and class hours. It may also arise because the status of one man has in some way been compromised by the appointment or promotion of another. This point has been amply illustrated before and does not need extensive discussion here.

In general, communication within departments is good, and potentially disruptive internal stresses are often held in check. Table 9.4 provides a kind of test of internal

Table 9.4

Comparision of Chairmen's Department Rating
with Peers' Department Rating

(N = 122 departments)

	RATING BY CHAIRMEN				
Rating by Peers	Among the first five	Better than average	Average	Poorer than average	Total number
Among the first five	37	9	–	–	46
Better than average	15	30	5	1	51
Average	3	7	6	3	19
Poorer than average	1	2	1	2	6
Total Number	56	48	12	6	122

communication by comparing chairmen's ratings of departmental quality with peers' ratings. It was expected that
chairmen would be more influenced by the Aggrandizement Effect than peers, since chairmen are more closely
identified with their departments than the rank and file of
department members. As the table shows, however, the
correlation between the two sets of ratings is high and positive, and the total distributions are very similar.[2] Ratings
between chairmen and peers are the same in 75 cases in the
table; in 29 cases chairmen rated departments higher than
peers, and in 18 cases, peers rated them higher than chairmen.

[2] Pearsonian $r = .94$, indicating that approximately 88 percent
of the variation in one set of ratings may be accounted for by variation in the other set, a *very* close association.

Stresses Between Department Members and Chairmen

One source of stress between the chairman and the members of his department is the Swivel Effect, which was touched on briefly before. The chairman's role has some resemblance to that of the working foreman in industry. In order to function as a chairman, he must represent management to the boys in the shop, and the boys in the shop to management. In the chairman's case, his orientation to his discipline usually puts him closer to the boys in the shop. The chairman's ability to carry out his duties, however, may depend on his closeness to management; and most chairmen, like most foremen, are chosen by management in the first place. To avoid imputations of disloyalty to his colleagues, he must conceal much of his contact with higher administration from the other members of the department. As a result of this uncomfortable situation, he tends to throw the responsibility for unpleasant decisions upward—especially the responsibility for invidious budget decisions which work hardship or sorrow upon individuals. Decisions with pleasant results he may attempt to claim for himself.

An example of what can happen when the chairman's position is *not* marginal is found below. Every university can show some comparable situation.

"The Chairman is an extremely authoritarian personality, and he's running a little dictatorship here. He is answerable only to the tenure members, you see, and there aren't any except himself. We, the junior staff, put up a united front to the Dean about the administrative inefficiency, lack of department meetings, and lack of clear-cut educational policy: we don't even have a clear idea of what the graduation require-

ment for a major is—he changes it capriciously all the time.
And treats us like dirt. But there isn't a damned thing the
Dean can—or will—do."

Perhaps a feudal analogy fits the position of the department chairmen better than a comparison with shop
foremen. A typology of common roles might run something like this:

THE ROBBER BARON.   Holding forth in a large and independently wealthy department, often of physical science,
the robber baron is an absolute autocrat within his domain
and a holy terror to the surrounding territories. He rules
his sovereign pincipality with an iron hand and wages aggressive warfare against his neighbors in an unceasing attempt to annex their budgets, if not their territories, and
to bring them under submission. He acknowledges only a
very loose allegiance to any larger political unit or over-
lord and often has the latter scared to death of him. He
spends most of his time behind his battlements, snarling
and planning future conquests.

THE LORD OF THE MOUNTAIN FIEF.   Like the robber
baron, the lord rules a large department; but, unlike him,
he is apt to be a benevolent despot, and his department is
more often old and prestigious than wealthy. He is often
a historian, economist, or linguist by upbringing, and he
prefers, from disciplinary bias and from taste, to retire behind his natural ramparts and let the world go its way
while he gently dominates his quiet valleys. He is a crusty
old bird, but no villain, and unobtrusive unless attacked.
Very frequently he is an elder statesman in campus affairs.

THE YEOMAN FARMER.   The pillars of the university's
workaday program, the honest yeoman and his plowmen
ask little except that they be let alone to raise their annual
crop of undergraduates and, in return for their inarticulate
allegiance, receive a small but just share of any spoils. Sel-

dom terribly exercised about anything except an immediate threat to his freehold, he toils in his fields with his
men and is distinguishable from them only occasionally,
when he speaks up to ask for another hand or a more equitable division of tasks.

THE GENTLEMAN ADVENTURER. A carefree and somewhat irresponsible sort, the adventurer is a latecomer on
the academic scene and wanders from realm to realm sing-
ing, telling stories, and doing well-sponsored contract research. When his record of being able to secure foundation
support is sufficiently gaudy to emblazon on his shield, he
becomes a chairman, and he is frequently picked up by
departments composed largely of brave but unimaginative
veterans in need of glamour and the repute of published
research. He eventually finds his way out of active teaching
and becomes an administrator. In his declining years, he
is sometimes called to be president of a small college.

It is easy to let the fun of making analogies run away
with us, but we shall run the risk a moment longer for a
hasty mention of three other common types of chairmen.
There is the Honest Burgher, the spokesman for the egali-
tarian, discipline-oriented department. Beloved by his department, well known in his discipline, he does not get
along with the administration, and as a result is constantly
interfered with. (Robber Barons like to characterize themselves as Honest Burghers.) A contrasting type is the King's
Man, who runs an authoritarian department through the
simple device of being hand-in-glove with the dean or the
president. He often has considerable institutional prestige
and no reputation at all in the discipline. Finally, there is
the Boy Ruler, usually an associate professor, who does the
work of the chairmanship for his elders while taking orders
from them. Although he relieves them of the chores of
administering the department, he is apt to be the ruin of

it, since he cannot get much done beyond passing out clerical supplies and arranging for graduate examinations. He
allows the elders to live in peace but is in no position to
press departmental demands upon the dean because he is
too much subject to the dean's authority. If the elders deal
with the dean on their own, he will become frustrated and
confused. If they do not, the department goes rapidly
downhill until it falls prey to one of the Robber Barons or
in desperation removes him from the chairmanship and
hires a Gentleman Adventurer to restore its strength.
Either way, he loses.

Turning from these not-very-ideal types, we note that
when stresses arise as a result of the recruiting process,
either within the department or between the department
members and the chairman, a simple and workable solution is frequently found in the senatorial courtesy principle
of giving any department member the right to blackball a
prospective recruit. Real stresses can arise within departments as a result of disordered status arrangements, and the
blackball can often prevent this disordering before it occurs.

Stresses Between Deans and Departments

Generally the faculty sees the dean as being less active
in the appointment process than he sees himself to be. He
has the prestige of the entire college to worry about, and,
since he has only one career (unlike chairmen, who have
two), he is often more identified with his college than the
faculty realizes. Additionally, he does promote and dis-
charge men—the latter unpleasant duty being thrown in
his lap by chairmen who do not want to be identified with
the negative aspects of authority—and as a result, he has
quite personal anxieties about doubtful appointments.

With regard to the academic payroll, the dean is usually the fiscal officer. (An astonishing number of replacements involve additional money for the department.) In no university in the sample are budget decisions made at the department level. Departments sometimes make their own appointments *when they already have the money for them,* but they are never allowed to appropriate new monies without the dean's consent. In some few instances, decisions on individual budget items are made at levels above the dean's, but normally he has final discretion in fixing the salary of a position.

The dean is thus closely concerned with the personnel process at both ends—appointment and termination. But, as he confronts all departments except the one from which he came (in which he is apt to interfere constantly), he finds himself facing a high barrier, for he is a disciplinary outsider and is distrusted as such. For his part, he often comes to regard department government as irresponsible and foolish, like the university's student government, and for much the same reason: most of their mistakes end up on his desk for rectification. After he has been a dean for a while, he is unlikely to give departments the benefit of the doubt.

But he has other problems, too. Like the chairman, he is a man in the middle and suffers from the Swivel Effect. His college as a whole must compete with the other colleges in the university for funds, and he is handicapped if he is the dean of an arts college, because his faculty are likely to be more imbued with distinctive academic *ethos* than the other faculties, and many of them deny his authority on principle. The faculty of a professional school is less likely to challenge their dean's authority, so that he is ordinarily able to speak for them without fear of contradiction or argument from below.

Popularity with the faculty is a doubtful merit in a dean. It is not uncommon for professors to rise to that position by leading local campaigns for faculty autonomy and then, once elevated, to grow into habits of despotism. It has been noted that deans often think *they* make appointments for their colleges, though they are handicapped by the fact that they are outsiders to all departments but their own. The personnel selection committee, whether *ad hoc* or standing, may be viewed in this perspective as a device to give the dean the final word on appointments while protecting him from the charge that he is a disciplinary outsider and not equipped to judge.

It seems to be true that most committee systems fall into disuse almost as soon as they are formed—*i.e.,* the committees accept departmental recommendations and let it go at that. The dean is aware of this laxness and permits it because he gains the right to intervene in a few cases where he wishes to do so. Departments seldom see the pattern of his policy, however, because from their limited observation the intervention appears to be capricious. Consider the following plaint.

"His termination: a matter not pleasant to recall, difficult to describe, not suitable for statistical treatment, better to be forgotten. A policy was there, but not clearly applied properly. It was a period of administrative turnover and deficit budgets. The dean's ad hoc secret committee said his teaching wasn't good enough. How would they know? I did say I was in a better position to judge that. From now on, I'm going to plan everything a year ahead and stick to the letter of the law. I'm bitter about it; it could have ruined the reputation of the department in the discipline. He could have been appointed."

This chairman's lament is easily matched with similar quotations from every university in the sample using the personnel selection committee system, for one of the surer penalties for a department which falls out of favor with a dean is to find him intervening directly or indirectly in its personnel process.

The respondents, it seems to us, tend consistently to overestimate the dean's power with respect to budget matters. They do not realize that the dean, too, sits on a swivel, and they are not aware of the consultation with higher echelons which he must undergo before he can hand down "his" decisions to them. Just as consistently, however, the respondents tend to underestimate the personal power which he wields over them individually. At one of the universities in the sample, a faculty member of any rank needs the personal approval of the dean to:

1. receive a promotion;
2. take leave without pay;
3. receive a sabbatical leave, explicitly defined as a privilege and not a right;
4. do extension or summer teaching;
5. travel anywhere on university funds or research funds administered by the university;
6. submit an application for a research grant;
7. accept a research grant;
8. employ any assistant or clerical aide;
9. order supplies and equipment;
10. be reimbursed for any expenses incurred on university business.

It is true that these requirements are ordinarily treated as formalities and are frequently handled by the chairman, but cases are cited in which the dean has denied permission for every one of the list of activities above, and in one or two instances, these means have been used for the systematic harassment of a senior professor.

The dean's power over *individuals* in the college is definite. His organizational authority over *departments* and their policies is distinctly limited and ambiguous. The fact that he can exercise power over individuals easily but over departments only with difficulty means that his control of departments comes to depend on his personal power over the chairman and other senior men, whose salaries and perquisites he controls. The personal nature of the dean's power is not often recognized, although it is widely resented. It may help to account for the active hatred of administrators so often expressed by professors.

"Administrators as a ruling class can be wonderful, or they can be aggressive and stupid. There's a kind of venality about them—not enough to compare with politicians, but they're of the same ilk."

"I have the feeling that the status of the profession is shrinking. And part of it is the increasing cleavage between the administration and the teaching staff. The representatives of the university that the public sees, who are they? They're the goons that need no training, the oily Hollywood liars, the alumni representatives and the public relations men. Who addresses the alumni meetings? Administrators! Public Relations people! The *athletic* department! When the universities —if they're state supported—take their requests to the legislators, who makes the presentations? Whom do the legislators see? Whom does the public read about? Administrators! Who knows what the faculty needs or wants or thinks? Who cares?"

Stresses Between Deans and Higher Administration

We have noted that the dean, too, is a swiveler. Like the chairman, he tends to deflect the responsibility for unpleasant decisions upward and to claim the pleasant ones for himself. When he speaks to those above him in the hierarchy he appears as the emissary of his faculty, but he may be Simon Legree when he turns his face to those below. We have no systematic data on the relationship between deans and presidents, but a number of interviews with presidents and provosts indicate that they also see themselves as active agents in the personnel process. As presidents look back upon their tenure in office, and as their official histories are written, they are likely to give a large place to their accomplishments in bringing men of high prestige to the university.

The relationship of the president to the dean seems to parallel in many ways the relationship of the dean to the chairman. In general, the presence of chancellors, vice presidents, provosts, and deans of faculties simply complicates the picture without effectively changing it. When we examine their roles, we see that they either assist the president in personnel matters or replace him entirely and free him, as in one of the universities studied, to be an ambassador from the university to the outside world. There are no other administrative levels which have much effect on the personnel process.

There is some evidence to suggest that the president, like the dean, sometimes intervenes actively in the recruiting process, especially in the case of major appointments, where he may conduct the negotiations himself. The legitimacy of this intervention is never questioned by our respondents, although it is often resented.

The trustees or regents of the university appear to play no part at all in the routine personnel process. They are frequently referred to as reviewing authorities, but there is no single case reported in which they took initiative or responsibility at any stage. This, however, has not always been the case.[3] Our sample does not happen to include any case in which the trustees played a part in the process of termination either; but as a number of well-publicized incidents show, they may be expected to participate, whether drawn in by presidents or deans, or acting on their own initiative, in terminations involving political or moral questions.

The Resolution of Stresses

Conflict in the university tends to be resolved in two ways: by faculty mobility and by the redistribution of authority.

On the department level, if we may judge from the reported duration of some department feuds, stresses are often not resolved at all. Instances are reported of fights which began almost twenty years ago and are still being carried on with great vigor, although all the original participants have departed from the scene. Exodus of the defeated faction may be the best solution; but even this, if it occurs slowly, is sometimes not sufficient, for departing members may have time to enlist new recruits for the fray they leave behind them.

The resolution of stresses between department members and chairmen frequently takes the form of a departmental rebellion. The typical outcome of such a rising is the departure of the disaffected members.[4] Most chairmen

[3] See Hubert Park Beck, *Men Who Control Our Universities*, New York, King's Crown Press, 1947.

[4] The following advertisement appeared recently in a professional journal: "Box 284. Available September 1, 1957. One complete and established department of geology and geophysics consisting of seven professors with Ph.D. degrees and six with M.S. degrees. Present positions have become untenable due to excessive teaching loads, lack of equipment, and poor salaries. Have hammers and coffee pots, will travel."—*Geotimes*, vol. 1, no. 10, April 1957.

enjoy the status of the chairmanship, cling to it, and do not relinquish it with grace. Since they enjoy some personal power over the members of the department, they are hard to unseat and are able to suppress most rebellions if they have the support, or even the neutrality, of the dean.

Rebellion against the dean is extremely rare, although bitter conflict between deans and departments seems to occur in all universities. Departments attempting such a move almost always fail, for the issues are usually department and not college matters, and one department rising alone is hopelessly isolated. The typical outcome of the struggle is either the resignation of the disaffected faculty members or the withdrawal of the department from the affairs of the college, if it is internally stable enough to accomplish such a retreat and retain its members. In the latter case, the department will probably be left unmolested, having shown sufficient strength to claim a measure of autonomy. At the other extreme, a department which complains that the dean meddles constantly in its internal affairs is probably one which lost a battle with him and which he was able to dominate thenceforth. The degree of autonomy enjoyed by a department or an individual faculty member is often an accurate index of their potential strength in campus feuds.

Presidents are even less subject to faculty recall than deans, and the adjustment of tensions between the two higher levels almost always takes the form of differential degrees of autonomy. The dean who is seldom seen in the president's office is probably a strong administrator who has won his autonomy, but since it is usually granted him under duress, his college may pay a price for it in financial support. The dean who is always in the president's office, on the other hand, is probably a weak administrator who maintains his position in return for doing exactly as he is told. That he may also be the president's friend is irrelevant, for the president is unlikely to have friends who have successfully threatened his authority.

Some Observations on Power in Universities

In order for any large-scale organization to carry out a complex program, a great deal of power [5] must be exercised. Decisions must be made, and men must be induced to carry them out. In most large-scale organizations, the distribution of power conforms, more or less, to a ladder of rank and authority and is supported by the formal assumption that rank and ability are closely correlated.

This kind of arrangement cannot be established in a university faculty because of the double system of ranking. Academic rank is conferred by the university, but disciplinary prestige is awarded by outsiders, and its attainment is not subject to the local institution's control. Everyone in the university recognizes, and almost everyone lives by, disciplinary prestige. Every academic rank includes men of enormously different prestige. Power cannot, therefore, be tied to specific positions in the form of authority, since such fixation would inevitably establish relationships of subordination and equality which were inconsistent with another set of social facts. Yet power in some form must be exercised or the university cannot function.

The solution to this dilemma which has evolved in the American university [6] is to let power lodge pretty much where it may. The fundamental device by which stresses in the university are resolved is a kind of lawlessness, con-

[5] "Power" is defined as the ability to influence the behavior of others.

[6] This is not the only possible solution; English universities have a different system and continental universities still another.

sisting of vague and incomplete rules and ambiguous and uncodified procedures. Thus it comes about, for example, that no written or unwritten rules govern the details of selecting professorial replacements in most of the universities in our sample. Within a single university, some new professors will be nominated by a chairman on his own initiative, others by the dean, others by a coterie of senior members, some by outsiders, some by formal majority vote, others by informal unanimous approval of the whole department or of its tenure members alone. This approval is ascertained, as the case may be, by individual consultation, casual conversation, or a scheduled meeting under parliamentary rules, and verified by a show of hands, a secret ballot, a signed ballot, or no ballot at all.

Being defined loosely, authority is allowed to roll free and is taken into whatever hands are capable of exercising it. It is not tied to specific positions for the reasons stated above and, additionally, because the tasks which members of the university must perform are so diversified and so complex that men *must* be chosen for them on the basis of their skills and not their amenability to supervision. Since this is the case, there is always a good chance that the occupant of any given position will be unable to exert authority or to submit to it. The system works, then, by distributing power in such a way that anyone who is able to exercise it may do so if he chooses. The product of this system is the university "strong man"—dean, chairman, or professor—who converts his prestige, either disciplinary or local, into authority by enlisting the support of the men around him.

That the system often entails considerable hardship for its weaker members has been shown throughout this report. But the powerless professor does have the protection of the tenure system to shield him from the capricious use of power by others—and the formalities of committee meetings to conceal and depersonalize its impact.

This system of loose-lying power helps to account for the extraordinarily high incidence of conflict reported in the universities we studied and the widespread and passionate dissatisfaction of professors with the workings of academic government.

Chapter 10

Current Trends
IN THE
Marketplace

Turning now from the internal stresses in the hierarchy, let us examine some of the trends in the wider marketplace and their implications for the future of higher education. Many respondents expressed a nearly frantic concern over the shortage of men which the academic profession as a whole seems to face. There were predictions of institutional collapse as a consequence of the problems of faculty recruitment which will have to be faced in the next decade. For the major universities however, the approaching crisis is likely to be softened by certain features of the institutional pattern.

In the fall of 1948 there were 2.6 million students enrolled in the colleges and universities of the United States. In the fall of 1957, there were about 2.5 million, a few less.[1] The number of faculty members[2] rose from about 196,000 in 1948 to about 250,000 in 1957. Faculties, for the most part, never contracted after the great peak of enrollment in the late 'forties, and hence little direct impact of the "tidal wave of enrollment" had been felt by 1957. Staff

[1] Estimated from various sources by the authors.
[2] Full-time equivalents.

increases were required throughout this period, however, as teaching loads declined from their traditional levels.

Professors in the major universities (as distinguished from many of their minor-league colleagues) do not usually have their work loads expressed in terms of a required number of teaching hours. With the improvement of their positions within the universities and disciplines, they have a tendency to shift their teaching loads to junior staff members.

Another significant trend of the past few years has been the shift of many student-related functions from professors to nonacademic personnel in the university's "civil service." Student counseling is an excellent example. Once a major part of the professor's job, it has by now been taken so much out of his hands that it received no single mention by any of our respondents as part of the duties of a faculty position.

A related point is that the changes in any university's enrollment tend to be concentrated in elementary courses, which are generally taught by instructors and assistant professors. An increase in enrollment in these courses necessitates the hiring of additional junior men, whereas enrollment increase in advanced classes would mean, for a while, a simple filling-out of existing facilities. When a graduate seminar, for example, increases in enrollment from two to ten (500 percent), this is apt to have no more significant effect than to cause the professor to spend a little more time listening to students and a little less time talking himself. In major universities, the linkage between student enrollment and faculty size is very loose. This is not the case in primarily undergraduate institutions.

It is not unusual for small colleges to tie their faculty size directly to student enrollment. Even the relative numbers in the various academic ranks may be determined by the distribution of students by class. For these institutions, then, any fluctuation in enrollment has immediate and significant effects.[3]

As shown earlier, most Ph.D.'s are trained in the major league. Most of them are hired, however, in the minor and bush leagues, since vacancies within the major universities themselves can absorb only a fraction of the Ph.D.'s who are graduated annually. What appears to be happening now, and what probably will continue at an increasing tempo, is that, as the major universities feel the need for additional staff, they will simply hire more of their own graduating Ph.D.'s. The shortage of personnel in the major universities is not likely to become acute as long as they can recruit from their own junior ranks. Major universities recruit instructors and assistant professors easily, since they control the wells from which the candidates are drawn.

The reader will recall the pilot study results (pp. 43-44) which showed the emergence of a negative correlation between the age and salary of full professors in one of the universities in our sample, demonstrating that the quickening of the market has had its greatest effects on the salaries of men in the mobile age ranges. It can also be shown that academic men are mobile for only a few years and that prestige is determined rather early in the normal career. The whole pressure for staff increases for all of the sectors of higher education, then, will come to bear on the lower ranks.

Major league universities have traditionally sent most of their graduating Ph.D.'s *down* the institutional prestige ladder. Logan Wilson observed that the academic recruit could not expect placement in an institution of higher

---

[3] Certain state college systems, for example, tie not only staff size but library, equipment, clerical, and supply budgets to student enrollment from year to year.

prestige than the one from which he was graduated.[4] The minor universities have also traditionally sent most of their graduating Ph.D.'s down the ladder to staff still lesser institutions. What is happening today is that the major universities are holding more of their graduates at their own level, trading them with one another and employing them at home rather than supplying them to the minor league institutions which, in turn, supply the bush league. This choking off of the supply of potential job candidates for the lesser colleges and the fringe employments of business and industry has resulted in greatly increased prices for the now scarce major league Ph.D. in these sectors.[5] However, we observe no shortage of personnel in the major universities, except in a few disciplines, such as mathematics and physics, which are suffering very stiff nonacademic competition. In the major universities, where there is little relationship between enrollment and staff size, there has been little response to the enrollment increase thus far. Wherever teaching is tied to enrollment and closely related to staffing, however, an enrollment increase calls for frantic recruitment, and the supply of men for the minor institutions is already tight.

We observe a tendency for wages to be raised from the bottom up, since it is the bottom ranks, and the bottom institutions, which are most responsive to market changes. Lower ranking institutions, then, are forcing salary ranges

[4] *Op. cit.*, p. 49.

[5] For an expression of this viewpoint, and for a statistical summary of the current situation, see *Teacher Supply and Demand in Colleges*, Washington, National Education Association (Research Division) 1957. Among other measures, the more extensive recruitment of women and of part-time college teachers is recommended. Additional statistical data are available in *Faculty in Institutions of Higher Education*, Circular #504 of the U.S. Department of Health, Education and Welfare, Washington, Government Printing Office, November, 1955.

up all over the country. Thus far, there seems to have been little pressure for expansion at the top of the hierarchy, and most of the openings for full professors are as replacements for full professors. The salaries of full professors are affected principally by their value to other institutions, but in the long run they are certain to be affected by the lessened reserve of major league personnel. Since there is a distinct tendency for the major league to increase the absorption of its own graduates, we can expect that the academic salary level will continue to rise most markedly for young men moving down the institutional ladder.[6]

This may have the effect of destroying the rank system within the minor and bush leagues. In the coming market, luring an assistant professor from the major league will cost a great deal. The professors already established in institutions at the lower prestige levels will not benefit equally. Their mobility is low, for prestige reasons; and even if it were not, they would have no place to go. It is to be expected, therefore, that the salaries offered new assistant professors in minor institutions will often surpass those of associate and full professors in place. Since no prestige can attach to academic rank in this situation, the hierarchy will probably break down, to be replaced by some sort of pay-range system similar to that of the elementary and secondary schools, with increments both for training and seniority.

The established professor in a major university can expect to benefit from the market situation in several ways. Since his prestige is a function of where he is known, and

[6] The case for a general increase of faculty salaries has been made many times in recent years and has now come to be generally accepted. For an excellent summary statement, which includes citation of the relevant literature, see Seymour E. Harris, "Faculty Salaries," *Bulletin of the A.A.U.P.*, V. 43, #4, December 1957.

the placement of his students in other universities is becoming easier, increased prestige is almost certain to lead
to increased mobility and to further increase in bargaining
power and its material emoluments. When most graduating
students were sent down the institutional ladder, the yield
in derivative prestige to their sponsors was low. With the
increased placement of students in other major universities,
the range of professional contact will be further widened,
with even greater emphasis on disciplinary rather than
local affiliations.

Increasing enrollment should also increase the number of major universities in the major league. This has
been true in other periods (Harvard and Yale were once
the only major universities in the country), and there seems
to be no reason why it should not continue. Graduate enrollments in the minor league may be expected to increase
for two reasons: first, because these graduate schools are
less likely to be filled to capacity than those of the great
universities and, second, because the ability of the great
universities to outbid the lesser ones will probably decrease as salaries for the junior ranks are equalized by the
market.

We should probably expect, as a corollary of this increased demand, that the individual professor will become
more autonomous relative to internal authority in the university and less subject to departmental controls. But as
mobility increases, the value of local prestige will decrease
even further. The identification of the strong men of a
faculty with the government of the university will become
more tenuous, and their opportunity to wield their power
will be lessened. This should lead to a corresponding development of the professional administrator, who has
severed all disciplinary ties or who is not an academic man
at all. The university's structure will probably diverge

even further from that of the disciplines than it does today. If university government becomes more independent of the faculty, many functions performed by faculty committees may be taken over by professional administrators and administrative offices.

To summarize these glimpses into a crystal ball, three predictions are hazarded on the basis of current trends: (1) a diminution of prestige differences among the major universities and an increase in the number of such institutions; (2) a widening cleavage between the major universities and the institutions chiefly concerned with undergraduate instruction; (3) increased differentiation between academic and administrative functions in the university.

In an effort to determine the extent to which opportunities for employment have increased recently, respondents were asked, "How has the job market in your field changed in the last five years?" The answers suggest that the changes perceived depend on the situation of the respondent. Those who are happiest with the current state of the market are the new Ph.D.'s. The junior men, in general, are cheerful about their prospects, whereas senior faculty members may be characterized as mildly gloomy, in part because the days of facile hiring are gone and in part because the market is better for their juniors than for themselves.

"It's better from the point of view of the prospective employee. There's a lot of demand from industry, government, and private research organizations. We've had one graduate student turn down offers of from $5700 to $6000 from good schools—assistant professorships—and he doesn't even have his degree yet. The top assistant professor in this department now only gets $6000."

There are a few disciplines where so many nonacademic jobs are available that they threaten a net shortage of professors. Some of these high-demand fields are experiencing a shortage of graduate students rather than degree holders, because men leave graduate work before the completion of their degrees in order to accept lucrative jobs on the outside.

> "It's harder to get people, especially in solid-state physics. The prices industry pays are going up every year. A firm in New York is offering $9500 for a new Ph.D. If we pay $5500 we're lucky. We really couldn't take a fresh Ph.D. and make him an assistant professor."

> "It was phenomenally good five years ago and now it's that to the fifth power. There is just nobody for the [academic] jobs, that's all, so they cut down the jobs. There wasn't any point in trying to find people—all jobs, no people!"

> "It's becoming consistently shorter—increasingly so each year. It'll get worse. There's a growing use of mathematics, and men are being pulled into industry and government at an increasing rate. Up until five or six years ago, all math Ph.D.'s from Princeton went into academics; they'd lose caste if they didn't. Now 50 percent go to government and industry. IBM is offering $10,500 to our boys before they graduate. One of our men, out just a few years, went into industry for $14,000."

This professorial crying-of-the-blues is not solely concerned with the problem of acquiring staff. In some fields, notably mathematics and physics, there is a growing concern about the supply and quality of graduate students entering the field. This is illustrated in the two quotations below. The first, from a physics department, is concerned with a possible shortage in supply; the second, from a mathematics department, complains vigorously about the quality of elementary training which students now receive.

"The need we anticipated developed in the summer of 1951 and has been growing with no end in sight and no indication of saturation. . . . Large numbers of our undergraduates are married now, and by the time they get their B.S., they've got kids and are feeling the strain. Since the offers are so good, it's difficult to stay and do graduate work. They all think they'll come back; none do. So the graduate enrollment is down, and what we have is composed of the lesser lights that don't get the really attractive offers. And, consequently, the demand for M.A.'s and Ph.D.'s is even greater. Industry needs graduates with advanced degrees—people need the degrees—but they can't get the information by themselves while working at a full-time job. They've got to come back and they aren't willing. It involves too great a sacrifice. And industry won't let them alone until they get the advanced degrees. It's a vicious circle."

"Mathematicians are in great demand, and that demand is going to increase. The rate of demand will also increase. I think that all of this is going to have a disastrous effect on mathematics in general, and on this department in particular. I think that it will deprive the undergraduate of mathematics. We won't have any teachers to give it to him. In one institution I know of, there was recently a proposal made to the faculty that the Math department grant the Master of Education in order to prepare teachers for the high school teaching of mathematics. They said they wanted to give the degrees themselves because they didn't want to waste their time teaching mathematics to people under the control of the School of Education. You can imagine how people reacted to that. So they aren't going to be able to teach it to them and those bastards will go on fouling up, making blunderers out of people who will then be turned loose to convince more generations of people that math is terrible stuff."

Statements of this kind—which are quite representative—support the contention that whether there is a short-

age of personnel in a discipline depends upon the nonacademic opportunities in the discipline. Shortages are cur-
rently felt in those fields in which the reserve of trained
men has been drawn into outside employment. In the
other disciplines, we were not able to find any sign of a
general shortage *at the level of the major universities.* The
pinch comes further down the institutional ladder.

> "As far as I'm concerned, there's been no change. The
> major universities can get top-flight men without too much
> trouble—for some completely mysterious reason. There are al-
> ways people around who are crazy enough to teach. The
> places without some research activities, like the small colleges,
> are in serious trouble, and it's going to get worse for them.
> The level of instruction in science in the small colleges has
> declined catastrophically."

What this respondent, and this whole argument, is saying
is that men who formerly comprised the labor supply for
minor institutions no longer have to descend the ladder.
One rather peculiar, and somehow comic, result of the
rapidly changing labor market is that second-rate departments, which were always able in the past to get men from
better schools and have now found their supply choked
off, accuse the major universities of "stockpiling" staff. We
discovered no evidence of this practice, and no department
admitted to it. As we have seen, the close connection between vacancies and appointments would not ordinarily
permit a department to do so, but the accusations are frequent nevertheless.

> "It's tight as hell and it's going to be tighter. It's definitely
> going to be a seller's market. Some departments are *stock-
> piling* people right now! I would, too, if I could. They're well
> advised to do so, because in two or three years there isn't
> going to be a man worth having in a school loose for a
> school to get."

Chapter 11

Discussion
AND
Recommendations

In the foregoing pages, we have attempted to describe the academic marketplace as a social system. Like most social systems, its pieces fit together, and its workings can be explained. To say this is not to say that it has evolved in the best possible way and could not be improved by rational planning. On the contrary, we submit that the practices which now prevail in the employment of scholars are needlessly damaging to individuals and to institutions.

It may be useful to summarize in one place some of the problems which come to view as we analyze the data. One man's frustration may, of course, be another's felicity, and an element of a social system may be functional for some parts of the system and disfunctional for others, but the existence of a problem for someone in a social system does not mean that someone else automatically benefits. Similarly, the solution of a problem does not mean that a new problem of the same magnitude necessarily appears in its place, although it must be admitted that organizational reforms are always likely to have unanticipated consequences.[1] It may be useful to divide this discussion into two parts—the problems of individual scholars and the problems of university administrators. Obviously the administrative problems of universities are of direct concern to faculty members, and the problems of individual scholars ought to be of paramount importance to universities, but the interests of individuals and institutions diverge in some respects, and it is convenient here to look at the same problems from two slightly different viewpoints.

Problems of the Individual Scholar

TEACHING VS. RESEARCH. Perhaps the leading problem for the individual faculty member is the incongruity between his job assignment and the work which determines

[1] A delightful exploration of the hypothetical consequences of an academic reform is George J. Stigler's "An Academic Episode," *A.A.U.P. Bulletin,* Vol. 33: 661-5 December 1947. This satire starts with the adoption by a South American university of a rule that in June of each year any member of the faculty can challenge the person immediately above him in rank to a competitive examination. The immediate results were favorable, but in the long run it was observed that faculty members were hoarding knowledge. Therefore, the regulations were amended to grant a bonus to a teacher for any of his students who won a challenge. Another unanticipated consequence appeared in the migration of graduate students to study abroad with the foreign professors who submitted the examination questions. A further effect was the interruption of research and the demotion of men who spent their time in current work instead of cramming. Another amendment was introduced, giving credit for publications, and making the calculations still more complex. ("Cimoor, whose father owned a publishing house, succeeded in getting out two books within the first year, and so influential was his father that many of the reviews were neutral.") At this point, many of the professors retired by the reform came back to climb the ladder with the aid of their previous writing. Finally, the whole scheme was killed by one more amendment—namely, that a man receiving an offer from another university might be awarded a permanent bonus of any number of points.

his success or failure in his own discipline. As we have seen, most faculty members are hired to teach students and to bear their share of responsibility for the normal operation of the university as an educational organization. These are the duties for which they are paid and which they must perform. Although in most occupations men are judged by how well they perform their normal duties, the academic man is judged almost exclusively by his performance in a kind of part-time voluntary job which he creates for himself. Not only does his career depend upon these supplementary efforts, but there is a tendency for his superiors to punish successful performance of the tasks for which he is hired. It is only a slight exaggeration to say that academic success is likely to come to the man who has learned to neglect his assigned duties in order to have more time and energy to pursue his private professional interests.

Although this inconsistency is most strongly felt in the early stages of the academic career, it continues to haunt the planning and self-direction of academic men up to retirement and beyond. It means, for example, that the best teachers in educational institutions, those at whose feet students come to learn, often restrict themselves to a minimum of participation in the educational process. It means, further, that a great deal of foolish and unnecessary research is undertaken by men who bring to their investigations neither talent nor interest. The multiplication of specious or trivial research has some tendency to contaminate the academic atmosphere and to bring knowledge itself into disrepute. The empty rituals of research come to be practiced with particular zeal in unsuitable fields, so that a published article is regarded as more valuable than skillful teaching in such expedient sciences as mortuary education and, at the other extreme of academic respectability, a research paper earns more prestige than a volume of criticism among professors of modern literature.

INSECURITY. It is generally agreed that intellectual performance is facilitated by a degree of personal security. This idea is embodied in the almost universal acceptance of academic tenure and the requirement of fairly long notice before a nontenure appointment is terminated. The notion that security is a special requirement of the scholar is based upon various grounds which are not easy to evaluate objectively—for example, the belief that professors are, or ought to be, unworldly men, unsuited to cope with problems of self-advancement in quite the same way as businessmen or officials. Perhaps more realistic is the perception that intellectual creativity is often cyclical and sporadic, so that an important piece of work may be accomplished unevenly over a long period of years, subject to inexplicable breaks and delays. As many studies have shown, the peak of creativity is reached early in some fields and late in others and varies also in unaccountable fashion from one individual to the next. The ideal of academic freedom includes the assumption that men working on the fringes of established knowledge will often dissent from the truths of the majority, will appear unreasonable, eccentric, or disloyal, or will be unable to explain to others their motives for pursuing a particular line of effort.

Beyond these specific reasons for believing that a high degree of security should be a part of the conditions of faculty employment is a more general theory which applies to the employment of civil servants and salaried professionals throughout our occupational system. The public-health physician, the salaried official, the employed artist, are held to have sacrificed the possibilities of high remuneration and conspicuous consumption which their talents might have opened to them in another occupation, or in the fee-taking sectors of their own occupation, in exchange for assured subsistence which enables them to pursue long-term goals in their work without distraction.

It is ironical, in the face of this consensus, that academic employment is often experienced as much less secure than comparable work in industry or private practice. There are three situations in which the academic man is typically beset by insecurity. They correspond in a general way to the early, middle, and late parts of his career. As the data have abundantly shown, there is a high level of both economic and emotional insecurity during the early stages of the academic career before tenure has been achieved. In a major institution, the odds against the promotion of an assistant professor may be five or six to one. This means that the majority of suitably qualified men must anticipate a notice of termination, a traumatic readjustment, and a new start leading quite possibly to a similar outcome. The probationary status of assistant professors becomes more meaningful when it is related to the previous stage of the academic career. As graduate students, they have been tested in many ways and over a period of years for intelligence, persistence, and conformity. The ordeal is sufficient to eliminate the vast majority of graduate students before they reach the doctorate. For those who survive, the habit of insecurity and a certain mild paranoid resignation are standard psychological equipment. These characteristics are often strengthened by the discovery that the criteria which they must meet as faculty members are quite different from those which they have learned to meet in the graduate school. Even their present experiences may not be helpful, for reasons explained in earlier chapters, since the unsuccessful candidate for academic advancement often is unable to discover why he is rejected.

In the middle stages of the academic career, the chief

source of insecurity is what might be called the lack of tenure in a status. Established statuses and established relationships are very frequently disrupted by the exigencies of the market. The bargaining advantage of outside candidates is such as to threaten, at every point of his career, the man who stays in one institution. Because of the intrigues of the cloister and the sporadic tyranny which appears in academic government, only the most eminent members of a faculty are safe against the withdrawal of privileges which they have come to regard as essential or protected against attacks on their prestige. In a profession dominated by prestige orientations, these can be intolerably painful.

The third characteristic situation is the rapid loss of bargaining power, personal influence, and independence which occurs near the midpoint of the normal academic career, as the professor loses the potential mobility which gave him some defense against local pressures. When this decline is gradual, and associated with the movement toward a peaceful retirement, it may be taken as the normal course of events. Often, though, it is abrupt and marked by dramatic incidents. As we have previously noted, there is a kind of reversal of normal seniority under current conditions, so that younger full professors enjoy unreasonable advantages over their elders.

INEQUITABLE TREATMENT.   The ideal of absolute equity is seldom achieved in any occupation, and it is not surprising that professors, like other men, are sometimes treated unfairly. Certain features of the university system, however, sharpen the impact of unfair treatment. Unlike other employers, who may legitimately base the preferment of their employees on seniority or the hazards of office politics, the university is committed to the ideal of advancement by merit. In a community of scholars, scholarly performance is the only legitimate claim to recognition. As we have seen in the foregoing pages, the academic marketplace as a system rests on the assumption that the worth of the academic man can be measured by the quality of his published work. This assumption is so closely woven into the fabric of higher education that, when men of inferior achievements are promoted over their betters, the resulting demoralization is not limited to the persons concerned but tends to affect the entire milieu.

The most striking inequities seem to arise out of the prestige system itself. The mechanisms which allocate graduate students to departments of varying prestige are far less accurate than those which allocate faculty members. The new graduate student has not yet done any professional work by which he can be judged. His previous studies furnish only the roughest indication of his probable capacity as a scholar. If he is one of those whose talents are slow in developing, his record may furnish no relevant information at all. The new graduate student choosing the institution to which he will apply does not usually have access to any current knowledge about the prestige system in the discipline. His choice, professionally speaking, is made almost at random.

Unfortunately, as we have seen, the initial choice of a graduate school sets an indelible mark on the student's career. In many disciplines, men trained at minor universities have virtually no chance of achieving eminence. Even in those disciplines in which the distribution of professional rewards is not tightly controlled by an inner circle of departments, the handicap of initial identification with a department of low prestige is hardly ever completely overcome. Every discipline can show examples of brilliant men with the wrong credentials whose work somehow fails to obtain normal recognition.

This situation appears to be worsening under current conditions. With more activity in the academic marketplace comes the tendency for more rapid advancement through the hierarchy, which, in turn, hastens the fixation of professional reputation. To the men trained in minor departments, and to those who stumble too far down the prestige ladder in their early job seeking, the tendency for reputations to be prematurely determined is an additional handicap. Only if the lists are kept open for half a lifetime or longer, do they have any chance of overcoming their initial disadvantage.

We have discussed in the foregoing pages the various ways in which personal characteristics may become a basis for discriminatory treatment. Women scholars are not taken seriously and cannot look forward to a normal professional career. This bias is part of the much larger pattern which determines the utilization of women in our economy. It is not peculiar to the academic world, but it does blight the prospects of female scholars.

Discrimination on the grounds of religion, particularly against Jews, secondarily against Catholics, and sporadically against Mormons, Unitarians, and others, operates as a selective factor in the predoctoral phases of the academic career and to a limited extent in initial job placement. Thereafter, it ceases to figure importantly, at least in the major universities and in the major disciplines. There is reason to think that religious identification is a far more important factor in the minor universities and colleges and also, as our pilot study suggests, in some of the professional schools.

Discrimination on the basis of race appears to be nearly absolute. No major university in the United States has more than a token representation of Negroes on its faculty, and these tend to be rather specialized persons who are fitted in one way or another for such a role. We know of no Negro occupying a chairmanship or major administrative position in our sample of universities.

Discrimination on the basis of political affiliation has been the subject of much discussion in the past decade and the central theme of a whole series of causes célèbres. As things now stand, there is wide variation in the tolerance accorded to senior professors who were formerly Communists, a tolerance depending upon the climate of the campus and the circumstances of the individual's recantation. However, it is plain that the net outcome of the prolonged crisis of academic freedom from 1946 to 1956 [2] is a marked restriction of the freedom of professors to engage in politics. According to some of our respondents, political activity of any kind by any faculty member is viewed unfavorably and is likely to bar or delay his advancement. Even when this is not the policy of the institution, it is likely to be construed as such by the junior faculty, with the result that there is extraordinarily little participation in politics by the rising young men of the current academic generation.

The more subtle forms of discrimination are difficult to describe, and we shall note them here only in passing. Our sample includes one case of a candidate who was rejected because of a mannerism in smoking which annoyed the chairman of the selection committee and many other instances in which the evaluation of a candidate was made on arbitrary grounds. Such incidents are perhaps inevitable

[2] The deterioration of academic freedom after World War II has been intensively studied by Lazarsfeld, under the sponsorship of the Fund for the Republic, in a large-scale interview study of 2,541 faculty members in 165 institutions. Paul F. Lazarsfeld, assisted by Wagner Thielens, Jr., *The Academic Mind: Social Scientists in a Time of Crises*, The Free Press, 1958. For a detailed account of nine cases in which professors were penalized for their current or former political affiliations, see the special issue on "Academic Freedom and Tenure," *A.A.U.P. Bulletin*, Vol. 44, No. 1, March 1958.

in an occupation in which merit is so much a matter of other people's opinions and so little susceptible to objective proof.

Indeed, the vast majority of personal problems reported in the interviews have less to do with long-range career opportunities than with the immediate working situation. The typical professor, if such there be, suffers from his acceptance of an ideology which is incongruous with his situation. He tends to see himself as a free member of an autonomous company of scholars, subject to no evaluation but the judgment of his peers. But he is likely to find himself under the sway of a chairman or dean or president whose authority is personal and arbitrary. For reasons explored in Chapter 9, academic authority is exercised largely by means of the personal control which the administrator has over the salary, rank, and prerogatives of the working professor.

This control is essentially illegitimate. It serves in default of a workable system of academic government. Like any improvised authority, it can easily become capricious. The assistant professor who offends the dean's wife at a party may be as severely punished for it as the lieutenant who offends the colonel's wife in a similar situation. True enough, with increasing rank and with permanent tenure, some of this helplessness in the face of authority disappears, but not before habits of obedience have been formed. Even a senior full professor can, as we have shown, be seriously harassed by his superiors, especially toward the end of his career, when it becomes difficult for him to seek another position. The violent opposition between the academic man's image of himself as a kind of oligarch, independent of lay authority, and the galling subjection which he actually experiences is presumably responsible for the combination of private resentment and public submissiveness that so often characterizes the faculty attitude toward administrators.

INADEQUACY OF INFORMATION. Among the immediate problems of the academic man as he moves through his career, the most striking and probably the most remediable is his chronic lack of information. There is no academic discipline, as far as we can discover, in which a listing of vacant associate and full professorships is available to a potential candidate. A few disciplines practice the listing of junior positions, but even in these it is not customary to list the "good" openings—those which carry more than minimum prestige or offer favorable opportunities for advancement. Except at the highest and lowest levels of the discipline, anyone seeking academic employment is ordinarily restricted to those positions which he happens to learn about from his friends and acquaintances. This is seldom more than a small representation of the positions available. As often as not, his choice will lie between undesirable alternatives while the position for which he is best suited waits around the corner for someone else. Moreover, the ban on open solicitation and the automatic depreciation of any candidate who shows excessive interest in a position mean that information about a vacancy may be unusable unless the candidate happens to have the appropriate connections by means of which his informal solicitation can be converted into an inquiry from the employing institution.

Along with inadequate knowledge of vacancies, the academic man is often burdened by a systematic ignorance of his own situation. In one of the universities in our sample, it is considered a serious violation of university policy for a faculty member to disclose his salary to a colleague. In another, the university budget is officially a public document, but most of the members of the faculty have never been able to obtain access to a copy. In a third, the bases on which a promotion is decided are held to be confidential and are not even revealed to the senior members of the department in which the promotion takes place. Quite literally, it is often impossible for a faculty member to discover his relative salary position, the opinion which his superiors have of him, the recommendations which have been made concerning his future, or the criteria on which his current performance is being evaluated.

Although sporadic efforts have been made in the various disciplines to develop comparative information, it is often impossible to obtain accurate reports on salaries, teaching duties, clerical and research facilities, or the normal requirements for promotion, as they compare from one institution to another. Indeed, even the most elementary personnel procedures in academic administration, such as the processing of recommendations for promotion, are often shrouded in a local fog of "security" which cannot be penetrated by the people most directly concerned. Over and above all these specific lacunae in the scholar's image of his own field of operation, there is a great conglomeration of myth and legend and a singular lack of straightforward analysis with regard to the workings of the marketplace. This book, in fact, is intended as a small contribution to this particular problem.

Problems of the University Administration

TEACHING VS. RESEARCH. The conflicting demands of teaching and research are felt as severely by the institution as by the individual. The identification of teaching with local prestige, and of research with disciplinary prestige, has been pointed out several times in this discussion. With the increasing emphasis on research and disciplinary prestige, the value of the local prestige which the university is able to bestow upon the members of its faculty tends to decline. This is likely to bring about an increasing orientation on the part of faculty to the demands of the discipline and the outside professional audience, and a progressive loss of interest in the curriculum and program of the university. Among the immediate consequences are the neglect of teaching, the devaluation of instructional tasks, and, perhaps most serious, the gradual erosion of the teaching responsibilities of the senior faculty.

The neglect of teaching is not a simple matter. It includes the failure to prepare good classroom lectures and lessons, an indifference to the results of teaching, increasing social distance between teacher and student (so that some professors never make the acquaintance of their undergraduate students as individuals), increased dependence upon mechanical methods of examination, and, at the worst, conventionalized contempt for the student. This pattern is discernible within every major university, but some institutions are notably worse than others. In general, interest in instruction seems to be best maintained in those undergraduate university colleges which are more or less autonomous and whose students enjoy some special status. The fundamental problem, however, is everywhere the same. Despite innumerable committees on the improvement of teaching, annual awards to the best instructor, and an intemperate eagerness in the colleges of education to develop courses in methods of college teaching, the alienation of the university faculty from undergraduate education proceeds apace.

The situation is considerably better with respect to graduate education. The graduate student is identified as a recruit to the discipline, and he participates almost from the beginning in research and related activities which are highly valued by the discipline. As he matures, his achievements contribute to the professional reputation of his sponsors. Only in a few of the largest and most prosperous departments, where graduate students are sufficiently numerous to lose their identity and the burden of graduate instruction is sufficiently great to threaten the working schedule of the faculty, is the graduate student regarded with the same ambivalence as the undergraduate. Unfortunately, this situation tends to occur in just those departments which are most attractive to talented students. It may even be true, as one often hears in departments of the second rank, that the best training cannot be obtained in the best departments because of their overcrowding.

The increasingly precarious position of education in institutions of higher education can be shown by such statistical indexes as the average teaching hours per week of senior staff members. In the two institutions whose statistics we have been able to examine, these indicators have fallen precipitously in recent years. Many factors contribute to the same result. The declining work week has been generally characteristic of salaried employments. The delegation of instructional chores to junior staff is probably a reflection of the increasing status of the academic profession and the increasing independence of its senior members. The gap between the teaching responsibilities of senior and junior staff members reflects, in part, the development of a host of part-time or interim employments—consultantships, fellowships, government assignments, administrative posts in the university—which are intended to be filled by the leading men of the several disciplines.

The basic trend away from teaching and toward research in the major universities is accompanied by minor shifts away from teaching and toward public service, away from undergraduate and towards graduate instruction, away from the general involvement of the faculty in the curriculum and toward specialization. The effects of these trends are mutually reinforcing. An increasing proportion of the faculty regard their teaching duties as obstacles to the performance of essential tasks, and instruction falls more and more into the hands of academics of inferior standing. This is not the place to discuss the emergence of new fields, such as General Education or American Studies, which attempt to redress the balance by adapting the departmental organization to a program centered on undergraduate instruction and to a staff without strong disciplinary connections. In some institutions, this innovation has worked out very well; in others, badly. In either case, there is no reason to believe that the interdisciplinary movement is more than a palliative for the general problem we have been describing. In the long run, the present trends will culminate either in the separation of undergraduate instruction from academic research—a development already visible in the increase of full-time research positions on many faculties—or the establishment of a new balance between the ever-increasing demands and rewards of research and the equally urgent demands of students to be taught.

INSTABILITY. The parallel between the problems of the individual and the problems of the institution is too striking to be overlooked. Corresponding to the insecurity experienced by the individual scholar is the instability of the institutional program which almost inevitably follows.

The borderline between appropriate turnover and excessive turnover is, of course, difficult to determine. Nevertheless, there is good reason to describe the present turnover in many institutions as excessive. Turnover is excessive when senior faculty members appointed to lifetime positions in connection with long-range programs leave after two or three years. With respect to junior staff, the expenditure of time and effort in recruitment is altogether out of proportion to the average duration of appointment for the people recruited. In qualitative terms, turnover may be reckoned as excessive when a university consistently loses members of its faculty whose services are needed and wanted and who cannot be satisfactorily replaced. The instability and loss of continuity in long-range projects, in graduate instruction, and the development of new curricula which result from excessive turnover can scarcely be exaggerated. A handful of very eminent institutions are protected by the fact that their tenure appointments are usually accepted as permanent. Minor universities are often protected against excessive turnover by the harsh fact that most of the members of their faculties have no other place to go. But for most major universities, the constant comings and goings of professors are a perpetual threat to planning and continuity.

There is a curious complication which haunts the sleep of administrators in these universities—namely, that the hazard of appointing incompetent or idle men to tenure positions increases as the general rate of turnover increases. Inevitably, a certain proportion of all appointments made are poor appointments. In the theoretical extreme case, in which all tenure appointees retained their positions for life, the proportion of "deadwood" on the faculty would be the same as the proportion originally appointed. However, when there is considerable faculty mobility, the ablest members of the faculty will tend to be the most mobile because of their attractiveness to other institutions, and the least competent members will tend to be immobile. For a weak major university, there is a real danger that almost all its superior appointees will eventually be lured away, leaving a permanent cadre which has been rigorously selected for incompetence.

ADMINISTRATIVE FAILURE.   There are a number of ways in which the workings of the academic marketplace contribute to administrative failure within each university—for example, by the internal dissension and low morale which follow the appointment of outsiders on unduly favorable terms. As we have seen, candidates for academic positions must normally be attracted from other positions of rather similar characteristics, and some bonus of rank, salary, or perquisites is expected in order to create a difference between the two positions. It is usually thought to be necessary to offer an outsider somewhat better terms as an inducement to move than an insider of exactly the same qualifications could obtain. As we have seen, this practice provides a perpetual incentive for everyone on the academic ladder to circulate among institutions. The result is a vicious circle, whereby the appointment of outsiders on unduly favorable terms causes dissatisfaction among the staff members in place, so that some of them seek their fortunes elsewhere, which requires more new appointments to be made by means of extra inducements, which has a further unsettling effect upon the remaining members of the staff. Meanwhile, the emigrants from this faculty going to their new institutions contribute to the same cycles there. It is possible to find departments which have remained in turmoil for decades through the operation of this mechanism.

A related consequence is the uneven growth or decline of departments or colleges within the university according to the fortunes of the marketplace. It often happens that a department loses two or three men in the same short period by sheer chance—for example, by the simultaneous occurrence of several retirements. When the persons involved are of high standing in the discipline, the fall in the department's prestige is appreciable, and it may result in a scramble of the remaining staff for positions elsewhere. In this way, decades of growth and development can be wiped out in a few months. The reverse process, by which sudden access to resources leads to a sudden spiral of growth, is much more difficult to provoke, but it does occasionally occur at the expense of the other university departments competing for the same resources.

Perhaps the most important problem of this type is the indefinite expansion and proliferation of course offerings and service functions, without much regard for the instructional needs answered, or the quality of the service rendered. Robert Maynard Hutchins has commented vehemently on this tendency.[3]

> "With transportation what it is today I do not see why every university should try to teach and study everything. Some subjects do not seem to me to have reached the teaching stage, yet we are ardently engaged in teaching them. Other subjects have not the staff available for instruction everywhere. Others can be adequately dealt with if they are studied in a few places. The present passion for cyclotrons seems to me excessive. The infinite proliferation of courses is repulsive. There is a good deal of evidence, I think, that the educational system as a whole needs less money rather than more. The reduction of its income would force it to reconsider its expenditures. The expectation that steadily increasing funds will be forthcoming justifies the maintenance of activities that ought to be abandoned; it justifies waste.
>
> "Some waste is inevitable; but the amount that we find in some universities is disgraceful. These institutions carry on extravagant enterprises that by no stretch of the imagi-

---

[3] *Freedom, Education and the Fund*, Meridian Books, 1956, p. 165.

nation can be called educational, and then plead poverty as the reason for their financial campaigns. The self-interest of professors, the vanity of administrators, trustees, and alumni, and the desire to attract public attention are more or less involved in these extravagances. Yet the result of them is that the institution is unintelligible, and, in every sense of the word, insupportable."

This problem is not altogether attributable to academic personnel policies. The numerous university self-surveys of recent years have shown a multiplicity of causes. Yet the connection between the academic marketplace and the proliferation of the curriculum is much closer than is generally realized.

The key to the whole problem lies in the fact that it is comparatively easy to add items to the program of a university and almost impossible to remove them once they are established. In the threadbare cliché of the faculty clubs, "No educational experiment ever fails." Almost every new faculty member is sooner or later allowed to add something to the existing curriculum or the existing program of services. This stands like a monument long after his departure. Chapter 7 pointed out why established courses and functions are regarded as poker chips in the perpetual game of budget distribution. When, to the rule which allows items to be added to the budget but does not allow anything to be subtracted, we add the probability that any existing function will develop into a vested interest, and when we further take into account the enormous distance which separates the modern university administrator from a close view of the departmental program in action, it is easy to understand the ameboid expansion of the curriculum and the shameless appearance of sinecures in the university budget.

IGNORANCE.   Like the individual, the university suffers from ignorance and poor communication in an increasingly complex situation which plainly requires knowledge and effective communication. The most salient feature of this ignorance is the inability of the department to obtain anything approaching a complete list of available candidates for vacant positions, or to determine the real availability of candidates under consideration, or to get accurate reports on current supply and demand in the disciplinary market.

Within the university, the problems of communication might well be placed at the head of the agenda for institutional reform. The haphazard character of university government, the prevalence of free-floating authority, the opportunity for intrigue which is created by ill-defined procedures and the habit of secrecy, and, perhaps most of all, the inclination of the working professor to dislike and despise administrators collectively while obeying them obsequiously in individual interaction—all these conditions impede the solution of the university's essential problems of how to discriminate between wise and foolish purposes and how to allocate limited resources to competing goals.

Recommendations

The recommendations which follow are put forth tentatively, in the hope of provoking further discussion. We believe, if we cannot prove, that some and perhaps all of the problems we have described can be ameliorated by any university which adopts a rational and restless attitude toward its own personnel policies. As a matter of fact, most of the measures suggested are drawn from the best current practice and can be observed in operation at one or another of the universities in our sample.

1. *That the tenure rank of lecturer be established for men primarily interested in teaching.*

The rank of lecturer might have two or three grades —for example, associate lecturer and full lecturer, corresponding to the associate and full professor and carrying the same tenure rights. It would be explicitly intended for men whose interests and achievements are centered in the instructional part of the department's program and who, in the normal case, do not identify themselves as research scholars. This might save for the university the scores of bright, energetic, and well-trained young men who are annually consigned to outer darkness for their unwillingness or inability to write research papers. At the same time, the plan implies that the precedence of research over teaching as a source of disciplinary prestige would continue to be recognized.

There seems to be no reason why the teaching responsibilities of conventional professorships ought to be reduced under such a plan, or why lecturers should be hindered in any way from engaging in research. Promotion from associate lecturer to full professor ought to be possible, although not routine. Similarly, transfer from a lectureship to a professorship at the same level ought to be possible, although rare. This innovation would abolish the rule that a record of published research is required for permanent employment in a major university. The recognition of achievement in teaching would be made a matter of routine occurrence.

2. *That the order of seniority at each academic level be respected and strengthened.*

The university should acknowledge the services which its faculty members render to it as an institution instead of rewarding only those services which they render to their disciplines. Increasing the value of seniority would tend to alleviate the problems now created for the professor as his potential mobility declines in his later years and to interfere with the mechanism whereby the market assigns a higher value to inexperienced and untried men.

Several specific measures are proposed. Seniority in all ranks ought to be recognized by small mandatory increments of annual salary over the base rate, in order to provide a financial incentive for long service and a decent minimum of salary progression for the older members of a faculty. It should become normal practice to respect the order of seniority whenever privileges or duties are to be distributed—for example, in the assignment of offices in a new building, the choice of courses for summer teaching, the selection of assistants, or the opportunity of a favorable class schedule. Seniority would normally run from the date of promotion, or by age if the date of promotion were the same for two colleagues. Although there are obvious dangers in the emphasis on seniority which prevails in railroading or the postal service, it is highly doubtful whether these dangers could arise for a university, since the importance of local seniority will continue to be limited by the countervailing attraction of disciplinary prestige.

The minimum operating principle involved in recognizing seniority is that no new recruit to the faculty ought ever to be hired at a higher salary or with more advantageous conditions of employment than any member of the same department who will be senior to him when he is appointed. The recognition of this principle would probably do more to decrease unnecessary and excessive turnover in academic departments than any other single measure.

3. *That standard base salaries be adopted for all academic ranks, and that salary information be made a matter of public and accessible record.*

This reform would strike at several evils at the same time. It would remove some of the uglier aspects of personal rivalry, help to neutralize salary as a status symbol, and thereby reduce the bidding power of outside institutions. It might diminish the invidious distinctions between departments which develop by historical accident on all campuses. It would sharply diminish the opportunities for personal advancement which now present themselves to the academic courtiers, the adventurers, and the semiprofessional nepotists. It would tend to reduce the personal control of administrators without in any way impairing their organizational authority.

Even though one of the institutions in our sample has successfully adopted a formula for standard and open salaries, the reaction to proposals of this kind, in both administrative and faculty circles, is often one of angry alarm. The usual arguments for differential salaries and for salary secrecy is that they facilitate the bargaining process and enable the university to obtain superior candidates who could not be attracted on standard terms, and to defend itself from raiding by meeting outside offers as they occur.

The findings reported in the foregoing pages enable us to assess the strength of this argument. This kind of differential bargaining appears to us to be unsound because especially attractive terms cannot be offered to outside candidates without creating an unending series of problems among the incumbent staff.

An auxiliary function of salary secrecy is to cloak inequitable treatment of individuals. We submit that a policy of strict equity may be the best reliance of the rational administrator in the long term.

4. *That a standard teaching load, expressed in class hours, be adopted in all departments of the university for all members of the teaching staff.*

This recommendation is put forward with considerable hesitancy and should, perhaps, be regarded as a suggestion for interim rather than permanent policy. The problems at which it is directed are the rapid and uneven erosion of the average teaching load in the major universities, the tendency for teaching to be delegated to junior members of the faculty, and the widespread practice of supporting research projects out of the funds intended for instructional purposes. This latter practice culminates, in some institutions, in the appointment of full-time research professors supported by tuition fees and other resources intended for teaching. This is not only unsound from an educational standpoint but it is altogether unnecessary. The normal organization of research in all the serious sciences is project-by-project. The typical successful project is individually designed, runs for a limited period of time, and uses personnel and equipment related to its needs. The full-time research appointee, lacking this framework, is very likely to drift into the role of the sinecurist. Our respondents sometimes complained of research professors, that they produced less research than the full-time members of the teaching staff.

These objections lose some of their force when the research program of an academic department has evolved into an independent research institute. This may, indeed, be the long-term trend. At the moment, however, no such trend for university research can be unmistakably demonstrated, and there seem to be advantages in the customary arrangement which combines teaching and research in the same department.

Adoption of a standard teaching load does not mean that all staff members carry this load in every quarter or semester. In all universities in the sample, there is now provision for the transfer of a professor's time from one budget to another. What this means in practice is that the man in charge of a major research project under outside sponsorship arranges to have the department reimbursed out of project funds for some proportion of his time. This money enables the department to employ a substitute instructor while usually retaining the services of the senior man for counseling, graduate instruction, and departmental participation. When rigorously followed, a procedure of this kind protects the instructional budget against diversion into research. Since in most fields there is now a flood of money for research, we see very little danger that research will be neglected in favor of teaching. All the hazard runs the other way.

5. *That both the period of probationary appointments and the period of probation be much extended.*

As we have seen throughout the report, faculty appointments are often made for one year at a time, occasionally for shorter periods, seldom for more than two or three years, so that decisions about reappointment or promotion must often be made before any real appraisal of the person concerned is possible. On the other hand, tenure—the right to lifetime employment—is usually awarded automatically to appointees at the higher ranks. It is likely to be obtained at an earlier age than formerly, and to be most valued by those who deserve it least. As we have seen, the anxiety and the excessive caution which characterize the recruiting process arise in part from the fear of appointing an unsuitable candidate for life. The unhappy solution is often to appoint him for so short a period that no real idea of his abilities can be obtained. Under current conditions, neither of these policies makes sense. Few qualified scholars are so flagrantly incompetent that their presence in a department for a number of years jeopardizes its reputation. Only a few scholars are so lacking in market value as to need a guarantee of lifetime employment before they have fully emerged from apprenticeship.

As we have shown, academic men in the major universities are highly mobile for about two decades after receiving their doctorates. Employment opportunities have been excellent for some years and promise to improve for a long time to come. There is virtually no problem of unemployment. Meanwhile, the increase of demand in the marketplace has lowered the average age for promotion to each rank and greatly increased the probability that tenure will be achieved before the individual's reputation is established. The need, then, is to re-establish the assumptions on which the whole tenure system is based—namely, that after some reasonable length of service, and upon the achievement of a secure reputation, a professor is entitled to the protection of lifetime appointment. This could be achieved, we think, by a double-barreled remedy. Specifically, it is proposed that no regular appointments to the faculty be made for a shorter term than three years, five years being ordinarily preferred, but that tenure not be acquired in any rank with less than ten years of full-time faculty service, including service on the staff of another university.

6. *That the fringe benefits of faculty employment be improved and expanded.*

Present practices with regard to fringe benefits for faculty members are unbelievably short-sighted. Because universities do not take into account the full costs of turnover, very few measures are developed to encourage staff members to resist the temptations of the market. Terms of employment are determined sometimes by business officers who identify themselves with the nonacademic employees and sometimes by deans who are more sympathetic to the needs of the students than to those of professors. Several of the universities in the sample have the curious policy that members of the faculty must not be given any privileges not equally available to students and stenographers. However laudable the motives behind this policy, it officially denies any special identification of the professor with the university. It also leaves out of account the special problems faced by the young faculty member as a middle-class professional with a lower-class income.[4]

Faculty fringe benefits are remarkably inexpensive for the institution which provides them in comparison to their value for the recipient. Many fringe benefits, like the right to attend classes without paying fees, carry obvious benefit to the university. A minimum list of such benefits ought to

[4] For a summary of recent evidence on the underprivileged income situation of the academic profession, see Seymour E. Harris, "Faculty Salaries," *A.A.U.P. Bulletin*, Vol. 43, No. 4, December 1957. For example: "In 1953, the professors in larger state universities, with incomes of $7000, were earning less than railroad engineers; associate professors in these institutions, less than railroad firemen; assistant professors and instructors, 24-30 per cent less than railroad conductors and switch tenders, respectively" (p. 586). Moreover, as Harris shows, nonacademic salaries *in the universities* have been rising at a much faster rate than academic salaries.

include family medical and hospital insurance and access to campus medical centers; unrestricted use of athletic and recreational facilities; a permanent waiver of tuition fees for professors and members of their immediate families; reserved parking on the campus; a reasonable retirement plan, to which the beneficiary is allowed to make extra contributions; mortgage loans for the financing of permanent housing (this enormously effective measure for holding staff not only costs the university nothing but earns a good return on investment funds); travel expenses to major professional meetings; and a well-appointed and nonexclusive faculty club. None of the universities in our sample provide all of these benefits. Two of them provide none. It is quite common for a university to charge a permanent member of its faculty at the same rate as a casual stranger for the privilege of parking near his office, or to deny him the use of university facilities which are available to every freshman.

7. *That the personal and arbitrary control of administrative officers over members of the faculty be reduced as far as possible.*

It is probably not necessary to repeat at this point that the reduction of personal control would not signify any reduction in the legitimate and necessary authority which administrative officers ought to exercise over the departments for which they are responsible. On the contrary, the uses and abuses of personal control which we have observed are best explained as improvised substitutes for a reasonable form of academic authority. The administrator's power over departments and colleges needs in many cases to be strengthened. His ability to harass and intimidate individual members of the faculty can only work mischief.

As things now stand, the salary-fixing privilege is the prin-cipal element in the pattern of personal control, but the practice of requiring an administrative approval for routine actions of all kinds also plays an important part.

Sabbatical leaves, for example, ought, if they are allowed at all, to be conceded as rights and not as privileges. It should not be necessary for the applicant to engage his own substitute or to satisfy the dean that the leave will "assist his professional development." Travel expenses should either be allowed to all or denied to all on the same terms. They should not be awarded subject to the chairman's decision that a given paper will "benefit the university." Procedures for promotion and for the achievement of tenure should be so clearly specified that these actions do not seem to the people concerned to depend upon anyone's whim. The procedures ought also to include the proper safeguards to assure that these decisions are in fact not made whimsically.

8. *That existing procedures for the location of candidates to fill vacant faculty positions be improved by increasing the amount of available information.*

This recommendation has several facets. There is a need, as we have seen, for wider circulation of information about vacancies to the field of possible candidates and conversely, for wider circulation of information about possible candidates to the field of prospective employers. Once this is accomplished, there is a striking need for improving the methods by which information about candidates is gathered for assessment and an equally urgent requirement that the time and effort taken to do this be decreased. Finally, something needs to be done to reduce the role of chance in the process of matching individuals and institutions.

The most useful device for increasing the amount of information available to candidates and employers would be to advertise vacancies publicly in the professional journals or by circular, and not surreptitiously or by private letter as is now the practice. The English universities have followed a policy of public advertisement for generations. It appears fairly certain that academic public opinion would be receptive to this experiment. Nothing at all is lost by open advertisement, except the opportunity to practice nepotism and the coyness which has become part of the employer's approach to the academic marketplace. This coyness is so deeply embedded in existing attitudes that the lists of vacancies circulated by professional societies in some disciplines do not identify the authors of announcements. Consequently they serve to arrange blind dates between individuals and institutions but do not give vacancies any publicity. The advantages of having a much longer list of prospective candidates, and of having them familiar with the terms of the position before they enter the roster, are obvious and considerable.

Once the candidates have appeared on the scene, there is a typical shortage of information about their actual achievements. The most elementary devices, consistently applied, could overcome this problem. For example, most universities do not have a standard application blank which is suitable for preliminary candidacies for senior positions or for candidacies initiated by someone other than the applicant. The scouting of candidates on their home grounds is not sufficiently practiced, often for lack of a budgetary precedent which would permit the members of a department engaged in recruiting to go to the candidates instead of having the candidates come to them. When the candidate is not widely known in his discipline, scouting is far more effective than the ritual visit, particularly if it is candid and open and includes interviews with the candidate's peers. In the case of junior appointments, offers should generally be made on the basis of the scout's report without further ado.

A substantial improvement might even be effected by the simple device of using the information in hand. Most of the regrettable or regretted appointments which now occur would probably be eliminated if it were formally required that *all* the professional publications of the candidate, including especially his doctoral dissertation, be *read*—not scanned—by a specialist in his field. Indeed, a written review of the candidate's publications ought to be an essential part of the dossier on which the hiring decision is made.

9. *That regular, orderly procedures be established for the selection of a new faculty member from a roster of candidates.*

Procedures of this kind can never be either regular or orderly unless responsibility can be clearly assigned. In the case of faculty appointments, this presents no theoretical problem. It is fairly plain that the professional qualifications of a candidate can be assessed only by his fellow professionals, and that this is the sort of situation in which more reliance can be placed on the judgment of a qualified panel than on that of an individual. In its aims, and even in its atmosphere, the evaluation of professional ability prior to a faculty appointment closely resembles the doctoral examination and is subject to some of the same rules. On the other hand, the actual appointment of a candidate to the faculty requires the exercise of powers which are not lodged in the department in any of the universities which we studied, and it has implications for the total university which cannot be overlooked. Current experience seems to argue for a procedure whereby the department *nominates* a single candidate and the dean or higher administration approves or vetoes the nomination.

The details of this basic arrangement may vary widely if the essentials are preserved. The nomination of the candidate should be a departmental matter without administrative initiative or intervention. The appointment of the candidate should always be reserved to the higher authorities of the institution and should not be subject to usurpation by the department chairmen and faculty cliques. Our data seem to suggest that the development of new committees and functionaries to diffuse the responsibility for appointments is almost wholly undesirable. Outside experts, interdepartmental committees, and advisory boards either serve as rubber stamps or fall into hopeless embroilment. The form of the department's decision, whether democratic or oligarchic, by majority or unanimous decision, by open or secret ballot, is probably not crucial. Nevertheless, the great susceptibility of academic organizations to feuds and intrigues argues in favor of fairly strict parliamentary forms. These include decision-making at formal meetings, duly announced and open to all qualified members; the right of any participant to have access to all the available information on the candidate; full opportunity for discussion; parliamentary procedure with respect to motions and secondings; and a secret written ballot. The equivalent safeguards for the appointing authority include the formal disposition of the department's official nomination, in writing, and with an explanation in the case of veto, as well as a right of appeal from the dean's decision to higher authority. Even though the procedure of appeal would probably remain inoperative most of the time, its existence would significantly affect the spirit in which nominations were made.

10. *That regular, orderly procedures be established for promotion and for the renewal of contracts.*

These procedures ought to follow the same pattern as procedures for appointment with regard to the division of responsibility between the department and the dean, including the careful examination of evidence, the use of parliamentary forms in decision-making, the formalization of the dean's approval or veto, and the right of subsequent appeal. The debatable questions do not have so much to do with questions of procedures as with questions of authority—for example, whether nominations and recommendations should ordinarily be made by the senior members of a department only, by all of the members who are senior to the position concerned, or by all full-time members. Nevertheless, in the long run, the sources of injustice and organizational chaos are probably to be found more often in the lack of definite procedures than in a poor distribution of the franchise.

Regardless of whether departmental appraisal of a candidate for appointment or promotion leans toward democratic or oligarchic consent, it is certain that decisions will often be unfair and unsound if they are taken in private caucus and not in open meeting. The objectives desired by advocates of increased faculty autonomy (that is to say, by all academic men) are best assured when everyone involved in the department's affairs has a full opportunity to be heard. Perhaps the most effective antidote against the frustration and resentment which often accumulate at the lower levels of an academic department is a provision that any member of a department can nominate any colleague of lower rank for promotion at any time, and that such nomination leads automatically to a full hearing by the department.

The theme of the foregoing paragraphs is central to this entire set of recommendations. The department is the essential unit of identification for the academic man, the area of intersection between the curriculum-centered system of the university and the research-centered system of the discipline. A scholar's achievement and promise cannot be appraised wisely except within the department concerned and cannot be appraised at all except by professional colleagues. From the standpoint of the university as a whole, the final decision on appointments and promotions ought very properly to be reserved to those who have responsibility for the university as a whole. When it comes to deciding between Dr. A and Dr. B, however, by measuring what they have done or what they are able to do, the higher administrator is totally unqualified.

This division of responsibility for personnel matters between the department and the university is conceded in principle and in substance by many university administrators, and there is nothing new or startling about it. It does lead to certain problems—as, for example, what should be done about the disorganized department which is no longer capable of conducting its own affairs. If departmental responsibility for the selection of candidates means that an incompetent department must be allowed to nominate incompetent replacements for its retiring members, or that a department made up of chronic alcoholics must be permitted to hire convivial drinking companions, then quite obviously the whole notion is intolerable. Such departments do exist. They are not even especially rare. Almost any university can show half a dozen departments which are seriously substandard and whose independence ought to be restricted. A more vigorous approach to the general problem of departmental bankruptcy is clearly needed. Any department no longer capable of conducting its affairs might be placed in a sort of receivership under the direction of a caretaker committee of outsiders from the same discipline, who would administer the department's affairs, and upon whom would devolve the right to recommend appointments and promotions. The term of such a receivership should be definite. It should not exceed two or three years, and it should not be renewable.

11. *That the existence of a faculty vacancy be established always on the basis of demonstrated need for a particular position, and never on the basis of automatic succession.*

In the course of this report, we have traced the process whereby the positions on a department budget come to be identified as vested interests of the department, never to be given up for the benefit of the college or the university. Multiplied by thousands of specific instances, the effect of this attitude is disastrous for institutions of higher education. When new needs develop in the university's program, they lead to requests for new positions which must be financed. But when old functions become obsolete, when educational experiments fail, when interest in a particular field of knowledge declines, there is no corresponding change in the allocation of resources. Hence the university's tendency to expand indefinitely in all directions and to be too extravagant for its resources or too poor to meet its most urgent goals. One of the remedies for this condition is to remove the privileged status of positions in which a previous incumbent has died or retired or resigned, and to put them on the same footing as new positions for which funds are requested because a definite and well-documented need can be shown. If all departmental requests to make replacements in the faculty are reviewed on the same footing as requests for totally new positions, then the questions to be asked before the canvassing for candidates begins are always the same: Is this position essential to maintain the instructional and research program in this subject? Does the university's program in this subject deserve continued support? Are there alternative uses for these funds which have a greater claim to consideration? What is the appropriate rank and salary for a position of this kind? These are the questions which normally concern the administrative officers of the university and which cannot be answered except in terms of a coherent administrative policy. This kind of judgment, and not the hopeless attempt to decide whether Dr. A is a better geneticist than Dr. B, is the proper business of provosts and deans.

Once the fundamental principle is agreed upon, the details of procedure suggest themselves. Establishing the need for a new appointment, whether in a new position or in a vacancy created by the departure of a staff member, involves the same division of responsibility between the department and the university as an appointment or a promotion. In a very similar sequence of procedures, it becomes the department's responsibility to specify the duties and other characteristics of the position which it desires to fill, and the administrator's responsibility to approve or disapprove. As in the previous recommendations, the object of this innovation would be to increase the power of the university administrator to shape the long-term destiny of the institutions, and to decrease his opportunity for personal rule. We believe, perhaps too hopefully, that the recognition of the academic department as the primary unit of identification, the recognition of the university administration as responsible for controlling the development of competing disciplines within a single framework, and the insistence on explicit procedures to hold each participant in academic government within the sphere of his proper competence will lead to a situation in which all academic men can live in greater ease and with more hope of achievement.

INDEX

The Academic Profession

An Arno Press Collection

Annan, Noel Gilroy. **Leslie Stephen:** His Thought and Character in Relation to His Time. 1952

Armytage, W. H. G. **Civic Universities:** Aspects of a British Tradition. 1955

Berdahl, Robert O. **British Universities and the State.** 1959

Bleuel, Hans Peter. **Deutschlands Bekenner** (German Men of Knowledge). 1968

Bowman, Claude Charleton. **The College Professor in America.** 1938

Busch, Alexander. **Die Geschichte des Privatdozenten** (History of Privat-Docentens). 1959

Caplow, Theodore and Reece J. McGee. **The Academic Marketplace.** 1958

Carnegie Foundation for the Advancement of Teaching. **The Financial Status of the Professor in America and in Germany.** 1908

Cattell, J. McKeen. **University Control.** 1913

Cheyney, Edward Potts. **History of the University of Pennsylvania:** 1740-1940. 1940

Elliott, Orrin Leslie. **Stanford University:** The First Twenty-Five Years. 1937

Ely, Richard T. **Ground Under Our Feet:** An Autobiography. 1938

Flach, Johannes. **Der Deutsche Professor der Gegenwart** (The German Professor Today). 1886

Hall, G. Stanley. **Life and Confessions of a Psychologist.** 1924

Hardy, G[odfrey] H[arold]. **Bertrand Russell & Trinity:** A College Controversy of the Last War. 1942

Kluge, Alexander. **Die Universitäts-Selbstverwaltung** (University Self-Government). 1958

Kotschnig, Walter M. **Unemployment in the Learned Professions.** 1937

Lazarsfeld, Paul F. and Wagner Thielens, Jr. **The Academic Mind:** Social Scientists in a Time of Crisis. 1958

McLaughlin, Mary Martin. **Intellectual Freedom and Its Limitations in the University of Paris in the Thirteenth and Fourteenth Centuries.** 1977

Metzger, Walter P., editor. **The American Concept of Academic Freedom in Formation:** A Collection of Essays and Reports. 1977

Metzger, Walter P., editor. **The Constitutional Status of Academic Freedom.** 1977

Metzger, Walter P., editor. **The Constitutional Status of Academic Tenure.** 1977

Metzger, Walter P., editor. **Professors on Guard:** The First AAUP Investigations. 1977

Metzger, Walter P., editor. **Reader on the Sociology of the Academic Profession.** 1977

Mims, Edwin. **History of Vanderbilt University.** 1946

Neumann, Franz L., et al. **The Cultural Migration:** The European Scholar in America. 1953

Nitsch, Wolfgang, et al. **Hochschule in der Demokratie** (The University in a Democracy). 1965

Pattison, Mark. **Suggestions on Academical Organization with Especial Reference to Oxford.** 1868

Pollard, Lucille Addison. **Women on College and University Faculties:** A Historical Survey and a Study of Their Present Academic Status. 1977

Proctor, Mortimer R. **The English University Novel.** 1957

Quincy, Josiah. **The History of Harvard University.** Two vols. 1840

Ross, Edward Alsworth. **Seventy Years of It:** An Autobiography. 1936

Rudy, S. Willis. **The College of the City of New York:** A History, 1847-1947. 1949

Slosson, Edwin E. **Great American Universities.** 1910

Smith, Goldwin. **A Plea for the Abolition of Tests in the University of Oxford.** 1864

Willey, Malcolm W. **Depression, Recovery and Higher Education:** A Report by Committee Y of the American Association of University Professors. 1937

Winstanley, D. A. **Early Victorian Cambridge.** 1940

Winstanley, D. A. **Later Victorian Cambridge.** 1947

Winstanley, D. A. **Unreformed Cambridge.** 1935

Yeomans, Henry Aaron. **Abbott Lawrence Lowell: 1856-1943.** 1948